The Story of Syrian Refugees

HOPE AND A FUTURE

The Story of Syrian Refugees

John M. B. Balouziyeh

HOPE AND A FUTURE:
THE STORY OF SYRIAN REFUGEES

ISBN (13) (hardcover): 978-1-68109-006-1
ISBN (10) (hardcover): 1-68109-006-6
ISBN (13) (paperback): 978-1-68109-007-8
ISBN (10) (paperback): 1-68109-007-4
ISBN (13) (Kindle): 978-1-68109-008-5
ISBN (10) (Kindle): 1-68109-008-2
ISBN (13) (ePub): 978-1-68109-009-2
ISBN (10) (ePub): 1-68109-009-0

Time Books™
an imprint of TellerBooks™
TellerBooks.com/Time_Books

www.TellerBooks.com

Iraq photographs taken with Canon EOS 60D and Canon EF-S 18-55mm f/3.5-5.6 IS II SLR Lens and Canon EF 50mm f/1.8 II Camera Lens – Fixed; Jordan photographs taken with Canon A3100 IS (standard lens); Lebanon photographs taken with Nikon D5300 and 18-106 (Zoom) Lens.

NOTE: Names and other personally identifiable information of refugees discussed herein may have been changed to protect their identities, safety and security.

Dedicated to Kayla Mueller (1988-2015)
who in delivering humanitarian aid
gave her life
to the Syrian people

There is no greater gift, no greater friendship than this.

About the Imprint

The mission of Time Books™ is to reintroduce time-tested values and truths to modern debates on political, economic, and moral issues. The imprint focuses on books and monographs dealing with society, ethics, and public policy.

The *Refugee Rights* Series™ of Time Books™ publishes monographs and treatises discussing the laws and public policies surrounding contemporary refugee issues. Complete your collection with the following titles:

- *Introduction to the Global Refugee Framework: An International Legal Perspective*
- *Palestinian Refugees and International Law*
- *Hope and a Future: The Story of Syrian Refugees*

Books by the Same Author

Principles of International Law, Vandeplas Publishing (FL, 2d ed.)

Fundamentos de Derecho español privado, Thomson Reuters Aranzadi: مجموعة القانون العام | The Global Law Collection | 全球法收集 (Navarra)

A Legal Guide to Doing Business in Saudi Arabia, Thomson Reuters, Westlaw Gulf (Dubai) (co-author with Amgad Husein)

United States Business Organizations, Springer Science+Business Media (Berlin)

Les Enfants des Rues au Sénégal, Éditions Biliki (Brussels) (editor)

Las sociedades mercantiles estadounidenses, Editorial Marcial Pons: Estudios Jurídicos (Madrid)

Table of Contents

PART II. THE CAMPS

APPENDICES

"When Home is the Barrel of a Gun"

by Warsan Shire[*]

I want to go home,
but home is the mouth of a shark
home is the barrel of a gun
and no one would leave home
unless home chased you to the shore
unless home told you
to quicken your legs
leave your clothes behind
crawl through the desert
wade through the ocean
drown, save, hunger, beg

No one leaves home
unless home is a sweaty voice in your ear, saying-
"Leave—
"run away from me now
"I don't know what I've become
"but I know that anywhere is safer than here"

---

[*] **Warsan Shire** is a Kenyan-born Somali poet, writer and educator based in London. Born in 1988, Warsan has read her work extensively across the United Kingdom, South Africa, Italy, Germany, Canada and Kenya. In 2011, she released her début book, *Teaching My Mother How to Give Birth* (flipped eye ltd.).

Acknowledgments

This book would not have been possible without the selfless contributions and support of so many individuals. First and foremost, I wish to thank my wife, Alexandra, for her unwavering support, especially as I traveled throughout the Middle East visiting Syrian refugee camps, sometimes absent for weeks at a time.

I am grateful to Amgad T. Husein, my supervising partner at Dentons law firm, for fully backing our firm's advocacy of Syrian refugees. From the day I first began working with Syrian refugees on a pro bono basis, he has persistently acted on the belief that Dentons has a duty to give back to and positively impact our communities. He never required me to make a business case for my work with Syrian refugees. He spontaneously offered to cover the costs of my visits to Syrian refugee camps and deemed those visits to be full work days, not leave days. I didn't even need to ask. He gave the project his full support because he believed that helping refugees was the right thing to do. It was that simple. For this, I am truly grateful.

I would like to thank many individuals at our partner organization, the Norwegian Refugee Council (**NRC**) for their help in making this project come together—first and foremost, Mario Stephan, NRC's Gulf Office Director, for having embraced Dentons' partnership proposal, for having believed in the value added to the NRC since the partnership was launched in 2014 and for having made countless introductions as the partnership grew beyond Jordan to other jurisdictions in the Middle East. Since Mario's launching of Arabian Perspectives, NRC's new Gulf Office Director, Abeer Shubassi, continues to give our partnership her full support. I also wish to thank Julia Herzog-Schmidt, Lebanon's legal coordinator, who assisted in my visits to refugee camps in the Beqa' Valley; the entire NRC-Iraq team for all of their assistance in coordinating my visit to refugee camps in Iraqi Kurdistan; the NRC-Jordan team, for substantial support in my visits to refugee camps and urban settlements in and around Amman.

I am also grateful to United Nations High Commissioner for Refugees (**UNHCR**) staff who facilitated my visit to Za'tari Refugee Camp, including Kilian T. Kleinschmidt, Za'tari Camp Teamleader at UNHCR and the former "Mayor" of Za'tari Refugee Camp, and Nasreddine Touaibia, UNHCR Public Information and Mass Communication Associate. I also wish to thank United Nations Relief and Works Agency for Palestine Refugees (**UNRWA**) staff, including Lance Bartholomeusz, Anwar Abu-Sakieneh, Nidal Ahmad and Wael Rabah, for providing me valuable information, facilitating my visits to refugee camps hosting Syrian-Palestinian refugees and handling permissions to visit refugee camps.

I would like to express my gratitude to all of the Dentons lawyers and support staff who have contributed to our Syrian refugee advocacy project. If I were to list all of them, I would certainly fill many pages. I would like to thank Joby Beretta, Chairman of Dentons' Middle East CSR Committee, for his entrepreneurial approach to assisting refugees. Over the past two years, Joby has reached out to colleagues in Iraq, Turkey and Colombia to expand the support that we are able to offer refugees and internally-displaced persons. Since we began this project in 2014, his generous advice, guidance and spontaneous introductions have allowed the project to grow to where it is today.

I would also like to highlight the contributions made by Haya Al-Motlag of Dentons-Riyadh, for all of her research assistance; Lara Saraireh and Haya Moubaydeen, of Dentons-Amman, for their research on Jordanian law; Elias Chedid, of Dentons' affiliate office in Beirut, and Nadine Naji, of Dentons-Doha, for their assistance on Lebanese law; Doğan Eymirlioğlu, of Dentons-Istanbul, for his assistance on Turkish law; and Eugenie Misheal, of Dentons-Dubai, and Caroline Konitzer, of Dentons-Toronto, for their constructive book design input. I would like to thank Safwan Moubaydeen, Jonathan Burns, Hussein Almoubaydeen, Abdulrahman Aflah, Fatma Makki and Krystal Williams for supporting this project in many other ways, including through research, making introductions, offering translations and making inquiries at embassies and with government officials. I also wish to thank Carolina Ramirez of Dentons' New York office for her inexhaustible energy in advocating for Syrian refugees.

My gratitude is owed to Dr. Karim El-Mufti of Université La Sagesse in Beirut for his detailed and valuable comments and corrections that resulted in a stronger manuscript. I also wish to thank Melania Jackson, my editor and steadfast ally, for believing in this project and for her thoughtful comments on the draft manuscript.

I would like to show my appreciation to David Tafuri and Ayal Frank of the US-Kurdistan Business Council for setting up meetings that enabled me to speak with officials of the Kurdistan Regional Government on Kurdistan's response to the Syrian refugee crisis. Meetings with Foreign Minister Falah Mustafa Bakir, Minister of the Interior Karim Sinjari, General Sirwan Barzani and General Mike Issa contributed an important political and military dimension to the Iraq chapter.

Finally, I would like to thank Dentons for demonstrating its commitment to corporate social responsibility in both word and deed. In addition to the extensive support it has provided to countless Syrian refugees and partner organizations in the form of pro bono legal support, Dentons has generously underwritten the cost of the research that went into this book. In more ways than I can possibly recount, Dentons has exemplified a commitment to corporate social responsibility as an integral part of Dentons' culture.

Abbreviations

CCW .... United Nations Convention on Prohibitions or Restrictions on the Use of Certain Conventional Weapons Which May be Deemed to be Excessively Injurious or to Have Indiscriminate Effects (Geneva, 1980)
CDHRI .... Cairo Declaration on Human Rights in Islam (1990)
CEDAW .... The Convention on the Elimination of all Forms of Discrimination against Women (1979)
CPHR .... European Convention for the Protection of Human Rights and Fundamental Freedoms (European Convention on Human Rights) (1953)
CPPG .... Convention on the Prevention and Punishment of the Crime of Genocide (Genocide Convention) (1948)
CRC .... Committee on the Rights of the Child
CRSR .... Convention Relating to the Status of Refugees (1951)
CSR .... Corporate social responsibility
CUN .... Charter of the United Nations (1945)
DG ECHO .... Directorate-General for Humanitarian Aid and Civil Protection of the European Commission
EU .... European Union
FAO .... Food and Agriculture Organization of the United Nations
FRY .... Federal Republic of Yugoslavia
GA .... General Assembly (of the UN)
GBV .... Gender-based violence
GC I .... Geneva Convention (I) for the Amelioration of the Condition of the Wounded and Sick in Armed Forces in the Field (1949)
GC II .... Geneva Convention (II) for the Amelioration of the Condition of Wounded, Sick and Shipwrecked Members of Armed Forces at Sea (1949)
GC III .... Geneva Convention (III) relative to the Treatment of Prisoners of War (1949)
GC IV .... Geneva Convention (IV) relative to the Protection of Civilian Persons in Time of War (1949)
HC IV .... Hague Convention (IV) respecting the Laws and Customs of War on Land and its annex: Regulations concerning the Laws and Customs of War on Land (1907)
HLP .... Housing, land and property
HRC .... Human Rights Committee (of the ICCPR)

ICARDA ....International Centre for Agricultural Research in Dry Areas
ICC..........................International Criminal Court
ICCPR ....International Covenant on Civil and Political Rights
ICERD ....International Convention on the Elimination of All Forms of Racial Discrimination
ICESCR ....International Covenant on Economic, Social and Cultural Rights
ICISS ....International Commission on Intervention and State Sovereignty
ICJ ....International Court of Justice
ICLA........................Information, counseling and legal assistance (NRC core program)
ICRC........................International Committee of the Red Cross
ICTY........................International Criminal Tribunal for the former Yugoslavia
IDP..........................Internally-displaced person
IFRC ....International Federation of Red Cross and Red Crescent Societies
IHL ....International humanitarian law
ILC ....International Law Commission
ILI............................International Law Institute
ILO ....International Labor Organization
IOM ....International Organization for Migration
IRC..........................International Rescue Committee
IS ....The self-proclaimed Islamic State (referred to herein as ISIS)
ISIL ....The self-proclaimed Islamic State of Iraq and the Levant (referred to herein as ISIS)
ISIS ....The self-proclaimed Islamic State of Iraq and Al-Sham or Islamic State of Iraq and Syria (the Levant)
ITS ....Informal tented settlement
JCLA........................World Bank-funded Justice Center for Legal Aid
KRG ....Kurdistan Regional Government
LCC.........................Local Coordination Committees in Syria
MSB ....Swedish Civil Contingencies Agency
MSF ....Médecins Sans Frontières
NAT.........................North Atlantic Treaty
NATO......................North Atlantic Treaty Organization
NRC ....Norwegian Refugee Council
NGO........................Non-governmental organization
NORAD...................Norwegian Agency for Development Cooperation
OCHA ....Office for the Coordination of Humanitarian Affairs (UN)
OHCHR ....Office of the United Nations High Commissioner for Human Rights
OIC ....Organisation of Islamic Coordination
OIP..........................Office of the Iraq Program (UN)

OPCW .... Organization for the Prohibition of Chemical Weapons (UN)
OPEC .... Organization of the Petroleum Exporting Countries
PA I .... Protocol Additional to the Geneva Conventions of 12 August 1949 and Relating to the Protection of Victims of International Armed Conflicts, 8 June 1977
PA II .... Protocol Additional to the Geneva Conventions of 12 August 1949 and Relating to the Protection of Victims of Non-International Armed Conflicts, 8 June 1977
PA III .... Protocol additional to the Geneva Conventions of 12 August 1949 and Relating to the Adoption of an Additional Distinctive Emblem, 8 December 2005
PoW .... Prisoner of war
R2P .... Responsibility to Protect doctrine
Refugee Protocol ..... 1967 Protocol Relating to the Status of Refugees
RSD .... Refugee status determination
SAMS .... Syrian-American Medical Society
SC .... Security Council (of the UN)
SDC .... Swiss Agency for Development and Cooperation
SICC .... Rome Statute of the International Criminal Court
SICJ .... Statute of the International Court of Justice
SIDA .... Swedish International Development Agency
SOHR .... Syrian Observatory for Human Rights
UDHR .... Universal Declaration of Human Rights (1948)
UN .... United Nations
UN-Habitat .... United Nations Human Settlements Program
UNCHR .... United Nations Commission on Human Rights (ECOSOC subsidiary)
UNCHS .... United Nations Centre for Human Settlements
UNCRC .... United Nations Convention on the Rights of the Child (1989)
UNESCO .... United Nations Educational, Scientific and Cultural Organization
UNFPA .... United Nations Population Fund (formerly the United Nations Fund for Population Activities)
UNHCR .... Office of the United Nations High Commissioner for Refugees
UNHRC .... United Nations Human Rights Council
UNHSP .... United Nations Human Settlements Program
UNICEF .... United Nations Children's Fund
UNRWA .... United Nations Relief and Works Agency for Palestine Refugees in the Near East
UNV .... United Nations Volunteers programme
USAID .... United States Agency International Development
USKBC .... US-Kurdistan Business Council
VRS .... Army of Republika Srpska
WASH .... Water, sanitation and hygiene
WFP .... World Food Programme

WHO.........................World Health Organization

Preface

I never intended to write a book on the Syrian refugee crisis. Yet in my travels throughout the Middle East, as I witnessed the sorry state of Syrian refugees in their struggle to survive, I felt compelled to tell their stories.

As an attorney based in the Middle East, I have witnessed scenes that would draw tears from a stone, scenes that have made the gravity of the Syrian refugee crisis terribly clear to me. In the streets of Beirut, I was astonished by the number of Syrian mothers cradling their infants, begging for money to buy medicine, some succumbing to prostitution, trading their bodies for loaves of bread. In Jordan, an infrastructure already strained with water scarcity and rising energy prices is now buckling under the weight of more than half a million Syrian refugees.[2] In Iraqi Kurdistan, countless refugees and internally-displaced persons have been reduced to eating grass to survive.

In my travels, I met orphans separated from all known relatives, innocent bystanders rendered limbless by bomb shrapnel, children who bear psychological and physical scars, widows unable to treat terminal illnesses and families whose breadwinners one day never returned home, never again to be seen, leaving behind a family unable to pay for food, medicine and shelter. I have met refugees that have been displaced multiple times—first from Homs to other areas of Syria, then back to Homs, and finally forced to flee Syria altogether. I have met Palestinian refugees who for decades lived peacefully in Syria, only to be forced to flee to urban centers or camps in Lebanon or Jordan. I have met young children robbed of their childhood, forced to work to survive, loaded with burdens too heavy to bear. Many of these children have only known human suffering. Theirs is a land marked by blood and gore, ruled by heartless, lawless men.

For countless refugees, the Mediterranean Sea has become a graveyard. One Syrian child whose small, lifeless body washes up on our shores is too many; 13,000[3] child victims of war is inadmissible.

---

[2] To a large extent, Jordan has been unable to keep up with an unprecedented influx of refugees. Intensified fighting between the regime and opposition forces in Der'ā in 2013, for example, led to a 331% increase in refugees within just four months. Matthew Barber, "Jordan Shudders Under 331% Increase in Refugees as Conflict in Dera'a Intensifies," *Syria Comment: Syrian Politics, History, and Religion* (21 Apr. 2013), available at <http://www.joshualandis.com/blog/refugees-in-jordan-increase-by-331-percent-in-four-months>.

[3] The Syrian Observatory for Human Rights (**SOHR**) reported 12,517 children died in the Syrian civil war as of October 2015. "About 2 million and half killed and wounded since the beginning of the Syrian Revolution," Syrian Observatory for Human Rights (16 Oct. 2015), available at <http://www.syriahr.com/en/2015/10/about-20-millions-and-half-killed-and-wounded-since-the-beginning-of-the-syrian-revolution>.

As I visited refugee camps in Syria's neighboring countries, I witnessed first-hand the challenges refugees face on a daily basis in their struggle to survive—shortages of food, medicine and other provisions, the inability to care for the sick, the daunting journey from Syria into surrounding countries—for many refugees, undertaken by foot, often carrying small children and the wounded and injured; sometimes undertaken in the bitter cold of winter.

These are the stories I felt compelled to tell. The result was this book.

In April of 2014, I travelled to Amman to attend a course on international law. While I was in Jordan, I arranged a visit to Za'tari Refugee Camp, just north of Amman. Having read about this colossal camp countless times in feature-length newspaper and magazine stories, I decided to see it for myself.

That visit changed my outlook on the Syrian refugee crisis. No longer was the crisis an abstract event only to be heard about through the media. Now, it was real. Having encountered a humanitarian crisis of this magnitude, I naturally felt a duty to act, to mobilize whatever resources I had at my disposal to alleviate the suffering of the Syrian people.

The initial fruit of my visit to Za'tari Refugee Camp was a partnership that I established between my law firm, Dentons, and the Norwegian Refugee Council (**NRC**), which provides assistance and protection to Syrian refugees in camps and in urban centers. Upon my return from Amman, I spoke to the regional management of Dentons about setting up a partnership to provide advice to the NRC on the legal protections offered to refugees in Jordan. Dentons' leadership enthusiastically embraced the proposal, and in the ensuing months, Dentons offered the NRC pro bono legal advice on Jordanian landlord-tenant regulations, evictions, deportations, birth registration and foreigner registration.

The success of this partnership eventually led to its expansion to Lebanon, Iraq and beyond. Today, Dentons offers the NRC advice on a pro bono basis on international and local laws that govern refugee rights across the Middle East. To date, we have advised on the laws governing housing, land, property ownership, nationality, statelessness, human rights, refugee rights, deportation and resettlement of Syrian refugees. As I write this book, Dentons continues to expand its partnership with the NRC, one that serves as an important example of how the private sector can contribute to the protection of Syrian refugees, one of the world's most vulnerable populations.

The more I visited refugee camps, the more I learned how much there was to discover. I learned about the special vulnerability that women face, both from the perspective of gender-based violence[4] and, for many, the

[4] The prevalence of rape in some refugee camps is made clear by the account of Rafif Jouejati, the English spokeswoman for the Local Coordination Committees in Syria (**LCC**), who referenced at least 60 victims of rape in a single camp alone who were carrying the offspring conceived by the rape. Sara A. Tobin, *The Syrian Refugee Crisis and Lessons from the Iraqi Refugee Experience*, Boston University Institute for Iraqi

Continued.../

dangerous conditions for giving birth in refugee camps. I learned of families unable to seek medical treatment or pay deposits that many hospitals require before doctors would even see them. I heard far too many stories of infants dying at birth due to wholly-preventable causes. In my travels to Iraq, I became aware of the 4 million internally-displaced Iraqi's who, in the shadow of the Syrian refugee crisis, barely receive media attention. Throughout the region, I discovered an entire lost generation of Syrian children, deprived of an education and opportunities to thrive in safe, secure environments.

As I peered across my camera lens at these innocent children, I thought many times of my own children. And I also recognized that had my own family not escaped Syria just one generation earlier, I could have been one of these refugees. I could have been the subject of this book, rather than its author and photographer; my own children could have been on the other side of the camera lens.

I also learned of the particular complexity of reaching a political and diplomatic resolution to the armed conflict, one which would end the civil war and allow Syrian refugees to voluntarily repatriate to and rebuild their country. The Syrian civil war is no longer merely an internal disturbance comprised of sporadic outbreaks of armed violence, one that can be quelled with legal reforms granting broader legal rights to a restless Syrian population. Rather, the Syrian conflict has become a complex proxy war between nations that recognize the National Coalition for Syrian Revolution and Opposition Forces as the legitimate representative of the Syrian people and those that support Bashar Al-Assad's regime. This conflict has thus pinned Western nations and the Arabian Gulf States against Bashar Al-Assad's allies, including Russia and Iran. In the midst of this proxy war, countless armed groups have infiltrated Syria, either in support of or in opposition to Al-Assad's regime, many of which enjoy financing and support from foreign governments.

Syria's civilian population has become the principal victim of this proxy war. Trapped within Syria or in the surrounding refugee camps, and with Western nations and Arabian Gulf States having limited their refugee resettlement programs, there is little prospect that the living conditions of these refugees will be alleviated anytime soon. The Office of the United Nations High Commissioner for Refugees (**UNHCR**) estimated that in 2015 alone, more than 10 million Syrians—half of the country—was in need of life-saving assistance. This figure is more than every man, woman and child in New York and San Francisco combined, or Dubai and London combined, or Berlin combined with Madrid and Rome.

As each visit to the refugee camps gave me a greater glimpse of the complexity of the refugee crisis and of finding durable solutions, I planned

---

Studies (2013), p. 12. To fully understand the extent of gender-based violence in Syrian refugee camps, the figure cited by Ms. Jouejati must be multiplied exponentially to take into account the millions of refugees living in other camps throughout the Middle East. Ms. Jouejati further commented that due to the prevalence of rape, the most requested medications in the camp were for birth control. *Id.*

further visits. The visit to Za'tari Refugee Camp gave rise to the visit to Jabal Al-Hussein Refugee Camp in Amman, which in turn inspired the visit to informal tented settlements in the Beqa' (Bekaa) Valley of Lebanon, which led to the camps of Iraqi Kurdistan, and so forth.

The result was this book, which tells the story of Syrian refugees, their living conditions, their rights under international and local law, the application of these rights, the discrepancy between law and practice, the prospects of refugee resettlement and local integration, the challenges that stand in the way of durable solutions and the fate of the refugees as Syria is further drawn into a protracted armed conflict, which is increasingly taking on an international character.

The Syrian civil war has divided a nation and triggered the greatest humanitarian tragedy of the 21st century. Syria has been torn apart by sectarianism, a virulent strain whose wanton and widespread destruction has known no limits. If we fail to act, an entire generation will grow up not knowing human compassion. If we continue to demonstrate indifference to the plight of the Syrian people, a generation of Syrians will normalize violence and indifference to human suffering.

The Syrian War also gives humanity a chance to act. We can demonstrate human compassion in a way that history has never known. We can restore human dignity to the victims of the conflict, seeking justice for the needy, defending the fatherless, pleading for widows, visiting the distressed in their trouble. We can undo their heavy burdens, free the oppressed and feed the hungry. We can open the doors of our homes to the poor and the vulnerable who have been cast out.

It is no longer possible to ignore the Syrian refugee crisis. The Syrian people are knocking, and before each of us is a choice. Do we open the door?

The purpose of this book is to raise awareness on the Syrian refugee crisis— the greatest humanitarian tragedy of the 21st century—and to shed light on the dire conditions in which millions of Syrians are living. Hundreds of thousands of Syrians are trapped in cities under siege and are facing extreme hardships, including shortages of food and clean water. Countless Syrian children are being deprived of an education and a chance to grow, develop and thrive in secure environments. Entire villages have been displaced without access to shelters and basic provisions. Countless orphans have been separated from their parents and known relatives and are wandering about like ghosts. An entire generation that should be learning and developing socially and emotionally has been instead isolated in camps, relegated to slums and forced to survive in destroyed cities, in many cases personally drawn into a conflict that will forever compromise their innocence. Meanwhile, the Syrian civil war rages on with no end in sight, spilling over into neighboring countries, destabilizing the region.

This study, focusing on refugee camps across the Arab world, explores the plight and vulnerabilities of Syrian refugees. My hope in writing this book is that it would inspire readers to get involved. Some might visit the camps themselves and share their experiences with family and friends. Others might support the many aid organizations that are struggling financially. Readers from the private sector might contribute to camps in any way they can—building schools, advising on infrastructure, setting up pro bono health clinics, proposing technical solutions, hosting workshops and trainings ... there is endless potential for partnerships with the private sector.

For many people, the Syrian refugee crisis remains an abstraction, as it was for me before I visited Za'tari Refugee Camp. I thus hope that by writing this book and recounting my first-hand experiences, I will help transform this abstraction into a concrete reality. I hope that readers will be inspired to act as a result of this book. Perhaps somewhere around the world, a teacher will read this book and as a result, will volunteer a summer teaching refugees in Lebanon or Jordan. Perhaps a sports league member will read this book and decide to organize a children's soccer camp at Za'tari Refugee Camp. Maybe a dentist will be inspired to pack up his equipment and volunteer a week of free treatment to a refugee settlement. A hospital might organize a shipment of bandages and other medical equipment to help treat the wounded. Perhaps an entrepreneur will donate a portion of profits to humanitarian organizations assisting Syrian refugees. Or maybe a charismatic personality will undertake fundraising on their behalf. Perhaps a parliamentarian will pick up this book and as a result, vote in favor of expanding his country's refugee resettlement program.

Day after day, while beheadings make headlines and war crimes reach new milestones, thousands of humanitarians go to work in Syria and its surrounding countries, relentlessly confronting all of the psychological challenges inherent to working in conflict zones, making personal and familial sacrifices to defend human dignity, save lives and to deliver aid and assistance where it is most needed, even at the risk of their own lives. It is my hope that by telling the story of Syrian refugees, readers will become inspired to act similarly.

In the poem "Reflections of a Sojourner," the poet, like countless others who visited Syria before him, reflects on Syria's magic. He writes of Damascus's parks and vibrant gardens,

> ... Where kite runners run free
> City of glowing nighttime fountains
> Where gifts are given liberally
> Damascus, whose people find Providence in all things
> And celebrate each new encounter
> You promote the life of the spirit
> You are a great city ...

While the voice and words expressed are unique to the poet's own personal experience, the sentiments expressed are not. Poets, journalists and other writers who have visited Syria have left with the same impressions of the country's enchanting culture, open-hearted people and rich heritage.

Today, conversations about Syria are divided into two groups: those who were able to visit Syria prior to the civil war, who reminisce with fond memories of the country and her people, and those that regret having been unable to visit Syria before the War left its indelible mark of destruction on the nation.

Some say Syria will never be the same. I am not of this camp. As one refugee at Za'tari Refugee Camp so poignantly stated, "the Syrian people are very capable. We can rebuild [Syria] better than before."[5] Though it may sound romantic, I believe the transformative power of redemption always triumphs over violence and destruction. Yet though it may seem out of tune to the modern ear, mine is a view that sees the world in a perpetual struggle, with good and kindness and decency always triumphing over cruelty. Such a view requires a great deal of faith and patience, especially when we are inundated with so much news of seeming injustice. Yet despite what we may see or hear, I never doubt that, in the end, truth and justice never fail. In Syria, I see the potential to rebuild a nation, to triumph over those forces that seek her destruction. In Syria, I see hope and a future.

Born to parents who emigrated from Syria to the United States, I first visited Syria as a teenager with my father. My travels to the historic cities of Aleppo, Damascus, Lattakia and Homs in many ways left an indelible mark on me. In these cities, I encountered a culture that was so different from what I knew in the West. In Syria, life was centered on family, relationships and community rather than jobs or careers. Syria was not a rich country by any means, but on her streets, I never encountered mendicants or the homeless. Families and local communities, rather than governments, took responsibility over the poor and afflicted.

Throughout my travels in Syria, I visited families that exemplified the virtue of hospitality. I was welcomed to homes with generous spreads of kibbeh and kebabs, varieties of salads garnished with fresh mint, platters of labneh, hummus and baba ghanoush, rainbows of dates, figs and olives and fresh-baked pita loaves, with steam rushing out when broken. Hosts would spend hours with their guests over meals, and would find any occasion to celebrate with music, singing, clapping of hands and the beating of the Arabic drum. Visits to family and family friends were often unannounced and spontaneous, but always welcomed with Arabic pastries, fragrant teas and potent coffee.

It would be difficult for me to forget the hospitality of the Syrian people, whose generosity invariably displayed a preference of giving over receiving, no matter how little the host had to give. It was a hospitality that time and again drew me back to Syria, culminating with my US State Department

---

[5] Interviewed in *After Spring*. Ellen Martinez and Steph Ching (Directors). Busboy Productions, 2016. Film.

assignment to the US Embassy in Damascus in 2010, just before the start of the Syrian uprising.

As I prepared the manuscript of this book, I reviewed journal entries that I wrote during my assignment as an attorney in Damascus. One of my November 2010 entries summed up my observations of Syria at the time. I remarked how in many cities of the world, streets are left barren following sunset for fear of crime and violence, but in Damascus, there was no such thing. I wondered if crime ever existed in the ancient city. I was unable to describe how pleasant it was on a Thursday evening to walk through the gardens and the public squares in Damascus, where one finds entire families sitting out together on lawns, listening to music, telling stories, roasting nuts and breaking bread together, right up into the morning hours. Friends met and greeted one another on the streets, with no fear of the "other," no fear of strangers. The entire cityscape was marked by genuine friendships and close-knit community.

How things have changed. Today, there are no quiet saunters under the Damascene moonlight without the fear of crime or violence. Every city has its rebel groups, its soldiers, its armed guards and militias. Homes and shops are bombed and then plundered. Today, five years after my last visit to Syria, many of the homes and cities I visited have been destroyed. The homes that remain standing have been left empty and hollow, their former occupants having fled, preferring refugee camps over air strikes and gunfire. The music, laughter and clapping that once filled their homes have been replaced by the unceasing din of bombs, bullets and blasts.

Though Syria is largely in ruins, my memories of Syria endure, giving rise to a hope of what Syria can once again become. It is with this hope to preserve and rebuild Syria, together with a desire to inspire others to take action, that I undertook to write this book. After all, a single image of three-year old Aylan Kurdi, drowned and washed up on the shores of Turkey, galvanized the world into action in September of 2015. Nilüfer Demir's photograph of that small, lifeless body, pummeled by the waves of the Mediterranean, shook the world out of silent indifference.

If this book could similarly mobilize actors to protect Syrian refugees, to bring healing to the sick, mercy to orphans and widows, comfort to those who mourn, and restoration to those bereft of hope, then this book would have fulfilled its purpose.

Part I. Survey of the Syrian Refugee Crisis

Chapter 1. Crisis Overview

A. A Refugee Crisis that No One Imagined

1. Introduction

In early 2011, no one foresaw that what began as peaceful demonstrations would descend into a downward spiral of war, violence and ubiquitous destruction that would claim more than 250,000 lives. Gatherings of civil society demanding greater political freedom would take a violent turn, growing into the greatest humanitarian tragedy since Rwanda. No one foresaw a civil war on the scale that we are witnessing today, with hundreds of children falling victim to chemical weapons; another 10,000 slain by conventional weapons; and over one million more children having escaped Syria as refugees.[6] Undoubtedly, these numbers are a shameful indictment on humanity.

Each year, the headlines deliver record numbers of civilian war casualties as the methods and weapons of war grow more savage—first landmines, then chlorine gas and other chemical weapons, then barrel bombs, cluster munitions, sieges, the intentional starvation of civilians and other weapons and methods of war that cause unwarranted and unreasonable suffering among civilians. We continue to read of armed groups deliberately destroying civilian property, employing treachery, using incendiary weapons in populated areas, executing the injured and prisoners of war, beheading children, crucifying captives and in other ways, egregiously violating the laws and customs of war.

In August of 2013, rows of still, lifeless corpses of Syrian children—the victims of chemical weapons—shocked the conscience of mankind. In September of 2015, an image of drowned three-year old Aylan Kurdi, washed up on the shores of Turkey, dominated news headlines. In January of 2016, images of starving civilians trapped in Madaya and other besieged cities in Syria outraged the human conscience. Parties to the conflict may soon need to resort to biological, toxic, nuclear or other weapons of mass destruction to maintain the shock value of their barbaric acts.

Five years ago, no one envisioned mass atrocities, heinous crimes and violence that would spill across international borders, transforming sporadic acts of violence into a sustained, international armed conflict. No one

---

[6] UNHCR, "The Future of Syria: Refugee Children in Crisis," UNHCR – UN Refugee Agency, available at <https://www.flickr.com/photos/unhcr/albums/with/72157638177114305>.

predicted that a broad coalition of militants would infiltrate Syria, leaving behind a trail of havoc and destruction. No one expected that today, the self-proclaimed Islamic State of Iraq and Al-Sham (or Syria) (**ISIS**)[7] would occupy and control more than half of Syria and Iraq, exporting terrorist campaigns so effective that even nations as far off as Egypt and France are not immune to the organization's bloodshed and determined butchery.

The Syrian civil war has triggered a humanitarian crisis of biblical proportions. At the time of this writing, 4.3 million Syrians had registered with UNHCR[8] and at least 7.6 million more had been internally displaced within Syria.[9] The four years that have elapsed since the Syrian civil war began in 2011 have produced more displaced Syrians than the nearly seven decades since the 1948 Arab-Israeli War have produced Palestinian refugees. Today, at nearly 12 million, there are more than twice as many displaced Syrians as there are Palestinian refugees. If the current trend continues, every Syrian will be displaced by 2019.

The refugee crisis has taken a toll on the economies and political stability of Syria's neighbors in the Middle East and has triggered Europe's greatest migrant crisis since World War II. Each day, hundreds or thousands of civilians cross international borders, and countless others are left behind, trapped in a violent cycle of retaliation between state forces and non-state actors. Innocent civilians remaining in Syria witness and experience egregious violations of the most basic norms of international law. The wanton and widespread destruction of property has become normalized in Syria, as has the taking of hostages, bombarding populous towns and villages, denying consent to humanitarian organizations' access to vulnerable civilian populations and the enslavement and sale of women and children.

---

[7] In mid-2014, ISIS changed its name and now refers to itself as the "Islamic State" (**IS**). Chelsea J. Carter, "Iraq developments: ISIS establishes 'caliphate,' changes name," CNN Middle East (30 June 2014). However, many global media outlets continue to refer to the group as "The Islamic State of Iraq and the Levant" (**ISIL**) or "The Islamic State of Iraq and Syria" (**ISIS**). *See* Elizabeth Jensen, "Islamic State, ISIS, ISIL or Daesh?" NPR Ombudsman (18 Nov. 2015). In referring to the Islamic State, this text employs the acronym "ISIS" because, at the time of this writing, it is the term most familiar to readers.
The descriptors "self-described," "self-declared" and "self-proclaimed" are sometimes employed herein when referring to the Islamic State. However, when such descriptors are omitted, it is not the author's intent to imply the group's legitimacy as either "Islamic" or a "State." Rather, the descriptors "self-described," "self-declared" and "self-proclaimed" are sometimes omitted stylistically to avoid unnecessary repetition and to maintain the book's succinctness.

[8] Syria Regional Refugee Response, Inter-agency Information Sharing Portal, Regional Overview, UNHCR, available at <http://data.unhcr.org/syrianrefugees/regional.php> (last accessed 10 Nov. 2015).

[9] Humanitarian Information Unit, "Syria: Numbers and Locations of Refugees and IDPs," U.S. Department of State (17 Apr. 2015), available at <https://hiu.state.gov/Products/Syria_DisplacementRefugees_2015Apr17_HIU_U1214 .pdf (last accessed 10 Nov. 2015).

The scale of the Syrian civil war is staggering. It has already dramatically reshaped demographics in the Middle East, having displaced hundreds of thousands of religious minorities, including Christians, Shia's and Yazidis in Iraq and millions of Syrians across the Middle East, North Africa, Europe and beyond. Today, more than half of the Syrian population has been displaced, a phenomenon almost without precedent in human history. Some experts comment that Syrian refugee settlements surrounding Syria will likely evolve into permanent cities, forever changing the demographics of the Middle East, reshaping the region as we know it.

As the war continues unabated, violence emanates from Syria, miring the world in further bloodshed. The Syrian conflict has already critically destabilized one of Syria's neighbors, Iraq. ISIS has demonstrated its devastating ability to export terrorism from Syrian and Iraq, whether in masterminding the October 2015 crash of Metrojet Flight 9268 in the Sinai Peninsula, the deadliest aircraft bombing since Pan Am Flight 103 in 1988, or in orchestrating the November 2015 attacks that left over 450 innocent civilians dead or wounded in Paris and dozens more in Lebanon. As the January 2016 Burkina Faso terror attacks, the November 2015 Radisson Blu Hotel bombing in Mali and 2013 Boston Marathon bombing demonstrate with terrible clarity, no nation is immune from the threat of terrorism.

The following commentary of Jan Egeland, the Secretary General of the NRC and former UN Undersecretary-General for Humanitarian Affairs, in many ways expresses the gravity of the Syrian refugee crisis[10]:

> "An entire underclass is being created across the region. Insufficient international aid and the policies of host governments make it next to impossible for Syrian refugees to live in the Middle East. Refugees are losing all hope. The seeds of future unrest are being sowed. Without an enormous investment in the Middle East to support refugees and host communities, and a shift in the policies that prevent refugees from obtaining legal documents so they can support themselves and their families, refugees will have no choice but to risk the often life-threatening trip to Europe or elsewhere in ever greater numbers. They will do so in the hope of a safer, better life, and so would you and I if we were in the same situation."

The civil war also carries serious food security implications for Syria and the broader region. For the first time in history, a request was made in 2015 to withdraw seeds from the Global Seed Vault, a collection nearly 1,000,000 varieties of seeds and samples that, for reasons of security, is tucked 150 meters into a mountain deep in the Arctic Circle, isolated from the risk of natural or man-made disasters. Historically, the Global Seed Vault was only ever entered by those depositing more samples, but in 2015, a request was made for the first time to remove seeds from the Vault. The historic request

---

[10] Preface, "Drivers of despair - Refugee protection failures in Jordan and Lebanon," Norwegian Refugee Council, *ReliefWeb*, available at <http://reliefweb.int/report/syrian-arab-republic/drivers-despair-refugee-protection-failures-jordan-and-lebanon>.

was made by a Syrian organization, the International Centre for Agricultural Research in Dry Areas (**ICARDA**). Unable to replenish its stock due to the Syrian civil war, ICARDA requested to withdraw about 38,000 seeds from the Vault in 2015.[11] This withdrawal request is but one of the many consequences of the Syrian civil war, one that has serious implications on continued food security in Syria and, potentially, the region and the world.

2. Survey of the Syrian Refugee Crisis

When the Syrian conflict began in 2011, many Syrians fled their country to shelters in neighboring countries expecting to return weeks or months later. Four years later, many find themselves still living in informal tented settlements or in refugee camps established by UNHCR or in UNRWA camps originally set up for Palestinian refugees that fled the 1948 Arab-Israeli War. Syrian refugees initially feared that they and their progeny would share the same fate as the Palestinians, many of whom have lived in refugee camps for more than 60 years. Today, however, millions of Syrians living in informal settlements or under ISIS occupation can only dream of living under conditions similar to those of their Palestinian counterparts; for all of the challenges and vulnerabilities faced by Palestinian refugees, they at least have access to fixed shelters and, to a large extent, to basic state services. The same cannot be said of Syrian refugees, too many of whom are living in improvised shelters, too many of whom have been kidnapped, tortured, imprisoned, enslaved, shot, raped and discarded like used chattels.

This book explores one facet of the Syrian humanitarian crisis—the more than 4.3 million refugees that have fled Syria's violence and aggression in search of safety. The book explores the Syrian refugee crisis through the microcosm of Syrian refugees residing in Jordan, Lebanon and Iraq, including at both formal United Nations-administered refugee camps and at informal camps set up by groups of refugees in countries where official camps have not been sanctioned.

Among the United Nations camps explored is the UNHCR-managed Za'tari Refugee Camp in northern Jordan. With roughly 80,000 Syrians making Za'tari their home, the Camp stands as Jordan's fourth largest city and one of the largest refugee camps in the world (the second largest by some estimates). It is home to the world's largest Syrian refugee population. Moreover, the book examines UNRWA-administered refugee camps in Amman, Jordan and Beirut, Lebanon. These camps, originally established by UNRWA for Palestinian refugees, have become home to greater numbers of Palestinian refugees who have fled violence in Syria. Many of these are refugees that have been twice displaced—first from Palestine and now from Syria. In addition, we explore informal tented settlements of Syrian refugees

---

[11] Dominic Dudley, "Accessing the Doomsday Vault: A seed storage facility deep inside the Arctic Circle is playing a vital role in ensuring farming in the Middle East ha a viable future," *MEED: Middle East Business Intelligence*, Vol. 59, No. 48 (2-8 Dec. 2015), p. 23.

across Lebanon, UN camps in Iraq and urban refugee populations across the Middle East.

The following map provides a basic overview of the Syrian refugee crisis. The numbers have grown since it was published in 2015 and these numbers refer to refugees registered with UNHCR or awaiting registration. The actual number of refugees is higher than these figures as not all refugees seek to register in their host countries.

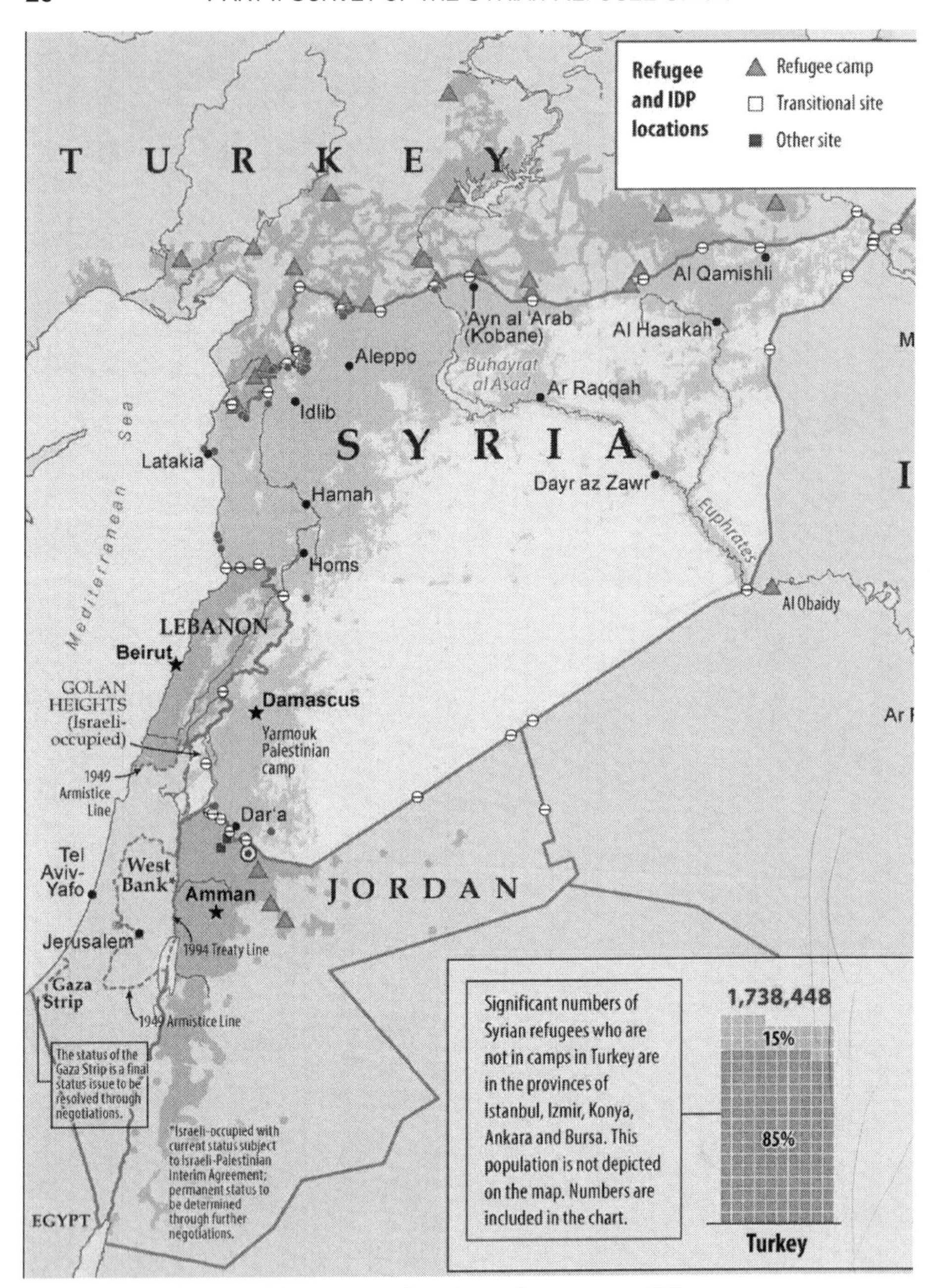

Figure 1. Numbers and locations of Syrian refugees and IDPs.

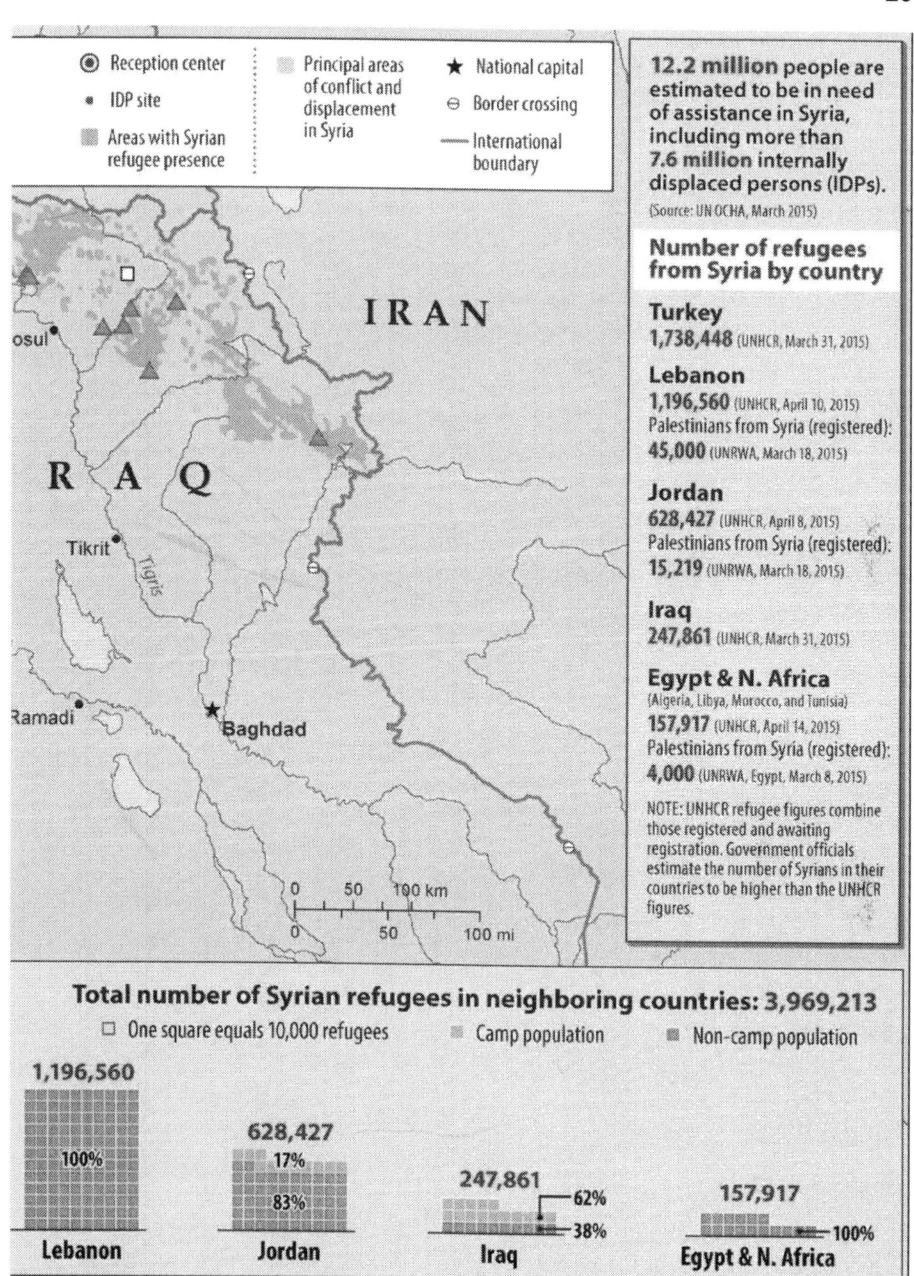

Sources: US Department of State (Humanitarian Information Unit), USAID, UN OCHA, UNHCR, UNRWA.

B. A Responsibility to Protect?

1. Introduction

Given the extent of Syrian's humanitarian crisis, many are left wondering: How can the international community stand by idly while women, children and other innocent civilians are slaughtered or rendered homeless by the millions? Isn't the international community under a responsibility to protect civilians from gross and systematic violations of human rights?

The question begs an answer, but no ready consensus exists. The Syrian government and its allies argue that an intervention absent the regime's invitation and consent would constitute an affront to the principle of state sovereignty and, absent a UN Security Council resolution authorizing the use of force, would violate the UN Charter and international law. Many prominent members of the international humanitarian community, in contrast, argue that the duty of the international community to protect the Syrian population from heinous crimes trumps the principle of state sovereignty. While interfering with the sovereign affairs of a State might contravene the letter of the UN Charter and damage the international legal order, they argue, failing to act while human beings are slaughtered would run wholly contrary to the spirit, principles and intent of the UN Charter. According to this argument, such inaction would render the international legal order immeasurably more unstable than would interference in state sovereignty.

In justifying their position, interventionists rely on the emerging doctrine that has come to be known as the Responsibility to Protect (**R2P**), which, they argue, would allow for the creation of safe zones, humanitarian corridors and other demilitarized zones in Syria to allow for the safe transit of humanitarian aid, whether or not the consent of President Bashar al-Assad's regime is obtained. However, as will be discussed herein, the legal basis that R2P supporters use to justify an international intervention is founded on shaky grounds. Their position would be substantially strengthened if they abandoned the R2P argument and instead focused their attention on the 1948 Convention on the Prevention and Punishment of the Crime of Genocide (**Genocide Convention** or **CPPG**) and other international treaties that clearly and unequivocally establish an affirmative duty to act.

2. The Responsibility to Protect Doctrine: A Brief Overview

a) Development

Given the experience of the 20th century, which saw countless episodes of genocide, crimes against humanity, war crimes and crimes of aggression go unpunished by the international community, a series of States and international organizations have come to recognize the R2P doctrine as an emerging principle of international law designed to protect citizens from egregious violations of international law at the hands of their own States.

Under this doctrine, the international community has a duty to intervene when a people suffers from egregious acts of violence at the hands of their State or as a result of their State's inability or unwillingness to protect its people. Supporters of the R2P doctrine argue that in such cases, the duty of the international community to protect the population trumps the principle of sovereignty of the State in question.

b) Controversy of the R2P Doctrine

The R2P doctrine, though increasingly recognized, remains controversial. One of the legal impediments to the universal acceptance of the doctrine and, more generally, to a military intervention in Syria is the principle of state sovereignty. Military intervention in a foreign State has traditionally been an affront to this general principle of law. Of course, there are cases under international law where invading a foreign State is justified, such as when such military action is necessary for a State's self-defense (*see, e.g.*, Art. 51 of the UN Charter). It remains, however, unclear whether there is a duty to infringe a foreign State's sovereignty for humanitarian purposes, such as protecting the foreign State's population against crimes perpetrated by the governing regime.

The legitimacy of the R2P doctrine remains cloudy and uncertain under international law. In a 2000 address to the United Nations, Secretary-General Kofi Annan recognized the inherent conflict between state sovereignty and the new, emerging R2P doctrine, which undermines state sovereignty. Acknowledging the atrocities of the previous decade, he asked: "if humanitarian intervention is, indeed, an unacceptable assault on sovereignty, how should we respond to a Rwanda, to a Srebrenica – to gross and systematic violations of human rights that offend every precept of our common humanity?"[12]

In response to Kofi Annan's 2000 address to the United Nations, the Canadian government formed the International Commission on Intervention and State Sovereignty (**ICISS**). In December 2001, ICISS concluded that when the State is unable or unwilling to fulfill its sovereign responsibility, "it becomes the responsibility of the international community to act in its place." On this basis, intervention does not contradict the principle of sovereignty, but rather complements it in situations in which the State fails to meet its responsibility.[13] The ICISS stated that on the one hand, "there will be damage to the international order if the Security Council is bypassed." On the other hand, there will be "damage to that order if human beings are slaughtered while the Security Council stands by." The ICISS thereby cautioned the

---

[12] Eve Massingham, "Military intervention for humanitarian purposes: does the Responsibility to Protect doctrine advance the legality of the use of force for humanitarian ends?," *International Review of the Red Cross*, Volume 91 Number 876 (Dec. 2009), p. 804.

[13] Payandeh, Mehrdad, *With Great Power Comes Great Responsibility? The Concept of the Responsibility to Protect Within the Process of International Lawmaking*, 35 Yale Journal of International Law 469, 473 (quoting *Int'l Comm'n on Intervention & State Sovereignty, the Responsibility to Protect* (2001) at 2.29), available at http://www.yjil.org/docs/pub/35-2-payandeh-great-responsibility.pdf.

Security Council that single States or coalitions might undertake action under the R2P doctrine if the Security Council fails to act on its own responsibility.[14]

Despite these pronouncements by the ICISS, R2P remains a deeply controversial and divisive principle of international law. Most prominently, the doctrine was used to justify NATO's 1999 military intervention in Kosovo. There, Russia vetoed United Nations collective security action under the UN Charter, yet NATO nonetheless undertook military action. Many observers today agree that NATO's actions were legitimate and legally justified under international law, but some argue that NATO's failure to secure a Security Council resolution damaged the international order, with the legal certainty that the UN Charter seeks to institute being the first casualty of NATO's invasion.

3. Duty to Act under International Treaties

a) *The International Covenant on Civil and Political Rights and Genocide Convention*

Some international treaties codify a clear to act within certain contexts in clear, unequivocal terms. For example, the 1976 International Covenant on Civil and Political Rights (**ICCPR**) requires that States agree not only to refrain from violating basic rights such as the right to life (Art. 6 ICCPR), freedom of thought, conscience and religion (Art. 18 ICCPR) and freedom of expression (Art. 19 ICCPR), but also that they ensure the protection of these rights from other member States' violations (Art. 2(3) ICCPR). Under Sub-Clauses (a), (b) and (c) of the Art. 2(3) of the ICCPR, States party to the ICCPR undertake:

> (a) To *ensure that any person whose rights or freedoms as herein recognized are violated shall have an effective remedy*, notwithstanding that the violation has been committed by persons acting in an official capacity;
> (b) To ensure that any person claiming such a remedy *shall have his right thereto determined by competent judicial, administrative or legislative authorities*, or by any other competent authority provided for by the legal system of the State, and to develop the possibilities of judicial remedy;
> (c) To ensure that the competent authorities *shall enforce such remedies when granted.*

The ICCPR thus not only prohibits States party from violating civil and political rights, but also, requires them to act to ensure the protection of these rights. It thus incorporates an affirmative duty to act.

Similarly, the Genocide Convention creates an affirmative duty to protect and "to liberate mankind from this odious scourge." It requires not only that its 140 States party refrain from carrying out the crime of genocide, but also that they "undertake to prevent and to punish" genocide (Art. I CPPG) and further

---

[14] Payandeh, *supra* at 474 (quoting *Int'l Comm'n on Intervention & State Sovereignty, the Responsibility to Protect* at 6.37).

pledge "to grant extradition in accordance with their laws and treaties in force" of persons charged with genocide (Art. VII CPPG).

b) ISIS' crimes as violations of the ICCPR and Genocide Convention

ISIS's persecution of Christian, Muslim and Yazidi minorities across ISIS-controlled territory in Syria and Iraq has been likened to genocide by legal commentators and international human rights NGOs. ISIS's own propaganda has, for example, characterized Yazidis as "Satan worshippers" worthy of death.

On 27 January 2016, the Parliamentary Assembly of the Council of Europe adopted Resolution 2091 condemning the acts of ISIS in the Middle East and characterizing them as genocide, war crimes and crimes against humanity. The Resolution declares as follows[15]:

> the persecution, atrocities and international crimes amount to war crimes and crimes against humanity; stresses that the so-called "ISIS/Daesh" is committing genocide against Christians and Yazidis, and other religious and ethnic minorities, who do not agree with the so-called "ISIS/Daesh" interpretation of Islam, and that this therefore entails action under the 1948 United Nations Convention on the Prevention and Punishment of the Crime of Genocide.

On 10 March 2016, religious leaders in Washington, DC presented the Obama administration with a 278-page report documenting genocide against Christians and Yazidis in Syria, Iraq, and Libya. The US Congress mandated for the State Department to decide whether to designate ISIS as a perpetrator of genocide against religious and ethnic minorities in Iraq and Syria. On the 17 March 2016 deadline set by the US Congress, Secretary of State John Kerry declared ISIS to be "responsible for genocide against groups in areas under its control including Yazidis, Christians and Shiite Muslims," having trapped, enslaved and killed Yazidis, "selling them at auction, raping them at will and destroying the communities in which they had lived for countless generations," executed Christians "solely for their faith" and "forced Christian women and girls into slavery."[16]

Moreover, ISIS' egregious breaches of international law constitute violations of basic rights protected under the ICCPR, including the right to life and freedom of conscience and religion. On this basis, the international community is arguably obligated under international treaty law to act to protect the victims of ISIS' reign of terror and ensure them access to effective and adequate remedies.

---

[15] European Parliament resolution of 4 February 2016 on the systematic mass murder of religious minorities by the so-called "ISIS/Daesh" (2016/2529(RSP)), ¶ 2, p. 5.

[16] Elise Labott and Tal Kopan, "John Kerry: ISIS responsible for genocide," *CNN Politics*, available at <http://edition.cnn.com/2016/03/17/politics/us-iraq-syria-genocide/index.html> (last accessed 19 March 2016).

4. Galvanizing Action through the Genocide Convention

As a result of the inability of the U.N. Security Council and the international community more broadly to come to a consensus with respect to the place of the R2P in international law, the world has remained deadlocked on Syria. Consequently, thousands of Syrians have been added to the number of displaced each week in their flight from the most brutal conflict of modern time.

The inaction of the international community will now likely change with the designation of ISIS' persecution of religious minorities in Iraq and Syria as genocide, thus triggering Article I of the Genocide Convention, which creates an affirmative duty to protect. Since the Genocide Convention, an international treaty and primary source of international law, is not fraught with the same legal uncertainty, ambiguity and controversy as the R2P doctrine, the obligations it establishes to prevent and punish genocide are binding upon the parties that have ratified it.[17] Nowhere is this made clearer than in jurisprudence of the International Court of Justice, which found in the Bosnian Genocide Case (*Bosnia and Herzegovina v. Serbia and Montenegro*) (2007) that Belgrade breached international law not by committing the crime of genocide but by *failing to prevent genocide* in the town of Srebrenica in 1995 and for failing to try or transfer to the International Criminal Tribunal for the former Yugoslavia those accused of genocide.[18] By undertaking their

---

[17] Furthermore, the Genocide Convention has been widely enough practiced among States that it arguably serves as a source of customary international law that, subject to reservations and objection, is binding on the international community as a whole.

[18] The decision against Serbia and Montenegro was not framed exclusively as an Article I failure to act; the International Court of Justice also examined whether Serbia and Montenegro had also committed genocide as defined under Article II of the Convention. The Court concluded that the 1995 massacre of over 7,000 Bosnian Muslim men in the town of Srebrenica (of the political entity Republika Srpska, within Bosnia and Herzegovina) was an act that satisfied the *actus reus* requirement of sub-clauses (a) and (b) of Article II of the Convention (killing members of a group and causing serious bodily or mental harm to members of the group, respectively). The Court also found that the Serbian forces acted with the requisite "intent to destroy … a national, ethnical, racial or religious group," as required by Article II. Therefore, the Court found that both elements of Article II (*actus reus* and intent) were met and the Srebrenica massacre therefore constituted genocide, as defined under the Convention.

However, the Srebrenica genocide was committed by members of the army of Republika Srpska (the **VRS**), which was separate and distinct from Serbia. The Court concluded there was nothing that could justify concluding that acts of genocide committed in Srebrenica were perpetrated by "persons or entities" having the status of organs of the Federal Republic of Yugoslavia (**FRY**) (as Serbia and Montenegro was known at the time) under its internal law, as then in force. Nothing suggested that the FRY army took part in the massacres or that the political leaders of the FRY had a hand in preparing, planning or in any way carrying out the massacres. The Court found evidence of direct or indirect participation by the official army of the FRY, along with the Bosnian Serb armed forces, in military operations in Bosnia and Herzegovina in the years prior to the events at Srebrenica. It was not, however, shown that there was

Continued…/

affirmative duty to protect, states party to the Genocide Convention will ensure their compliance with international law while also protecting the victims of the 21st century's most heinous crimes.

---

any such participation in relation to the Srebrenica genocide. Further, neither the Republika Srpska, nor the VRS (its army) were de jure organs of the FRY, since none of them had the status of organ of that State under its internal law.
Therefore, Serbia and Montenegro was not held responsible for the Srebrenica genocide. Rather, Belgrade breached the Genocide Convention by failing to prevent the Srebrenica genocide.

Chapter 2. The Global Refugee Framework: An International Legal Overview

A. Overview

After World War II, the international community was faced with the task of organizing thousands of displaced persons. There was a concerted effort to ensure that the atrocities committed during the war would never be repeated and part of this was achieved by adopting the Universal Declaration of Human Rights (**UDHR**) (1948). In order to secure the fundamental human rights of refugees, the Office of the UN High Commissioner for Refugees (**UNHCR**) was established on 14 December 1950. Headquartered in Geneva, Switzerland, the agency is mandated with the task of supervising international conventions providing for the protection of refugees. The main principle behind UNHCR and refugee law in general is to provide surrogate international protection for an individual where national protection of his fundamental rights has failed.

The primary mission of UNHCR is to promote the protection of refugees. Its role varies greatly from country to country, depending on several factors, including whether:

- there exists national legislation protecting the rights of refugees and national agencies or non-governmental organizations (**NGOs**) acting as refugee administrators;
- UNHCR is the primary refugee administrator or is even welcomed in the host country as an international presence.

While UNHCR does provide assistance and aid to refugees, its first priority is to advocate for the rights of refugees in host countries. It also encourages the development of national legislation that recognizes the rights of refugees and leads to a fair administration of those rights by national refugee agencies.

UNHCR may support refugees at the request of States or the UN itself. It assists in the local integration or resettlement of refugees into third countries as well as their voluntary repatriation to their country of origin.

UNHCR does not deal with the intake process of those who have already left their countries of residence. Such individuals may be welcomed by third party host states as asylees under local asylum laws. For example, the US permits any person who is already in the US or is entering the US to apply to remain in the US as an asylee. Under US law, the applicant must show that he has a reasonable fear of persecution because of race, religion, nationality, membership in a particular social group or political opinion, if forced to return to his country of last residence. Other States may apply a different set of criteria when evaluating whether to grant the right of asylum within its territory.

B. Convention Relating to the Status of Refugees

1. Introduction

The Convention Relating to the Status of Refugees (**CRSR**) was approved at the UN Conference of Plenipotentiaries on the Status of Refugees and Stateless Persons on 28 July 1951. The CRSR entered into force in 1954 and was amended by the 1967 Protocol Relating to the Status of Refugees. With 147 States party to either the Convention or its Protocol, the principles contained in the Convention and its Protocol now form part of customary international law.

The CRSR is in many ways a human rights convention in that it seeks to provide protection to any person who owing to "fear of being persecuted for reasons of race, religion, nationality, membership of a particular social group or political opinion, is outside the country of his nationality and is unable, or owing to such fear, is unwilling to avail himself of the protection of that country" (Art. 1.A(2) CRSR). The CRSR provides such persons the right of asylum in States party to the Convention and guarantees their rights to favorable conditions for gainful employment and for the practice of the liberal professions, housing, public education and access to public relief, among other rights.

2. The Convention Relating to the Status of Refugees and UNHCR

The CRSR was adopted in 1951, the year following the 1950 establishment of UNHCR. The Convention is central to the activities of UNHCR by defining who is a refugee, setting out their rights and outlining the responsibilities of the international community in applying refugee protections.

3. Definition of "Refugee"

a) Overview

Under Article 1 of the Convention, as modified by Article 1.2 of the Protocol, a refugee is any person who (Art. 1.A(2) CRSR):

> owing to well-founded fear of being persecuted for reasons of race, religion, nationality, membership of a particular social group or political opinion, is *outside the country of his nationality* and is unable, or owing to such fear, is unwilling to avail himself of the protection of that country; or who, not having a nationality and being outside the country of his former habitual residence as a result of such events, is unable or, owing to such fear, is unwilling to return to it.

There are thus two key elements to the definition of a "refugee" under the CRSR:

- The person must be *outside of his country* or nationality or habitual residence (*i.e.*, an international border must have been crossed); and
- The reason for the person's displacement is a *well-founded fear of persecution* for reasons of race, religion, nationality, membership of a particular social group or political opinion.

Several regional conventions have expanded this definition by including persons compelled to leave their country owing to generalized violence and aggression (*see, e.g.*, "Organization of African Unity Convention (1969)" and "Cartagena Declaration (1984)" under "Regional Conventions," *infra.*).

Article 1 also sets forth a series of exceptions to the general definition of "refugee" provided above. Even if there is a well-founded fear of persecution for reasons of race, religion, nationality, membership of a social group or political opinion, the following individuals may not seek refugee status:

- An individual who (1) has voluntarily re-availed himself of the protection of the country of his nationality; (2) having lost his nationality, has voluntarily reacquired it; (3) has acquired a new nationality and enjoys the protection of the country of his new nationality; (4) has voluntarily re-established himself in the country which he left or outside which he remained owing to fear of persecution; or (5) can no longer, because the circumstances in connection with which he has been recognized as a refugee have ceased to exist, continue to refuse to avail himself of the protection of the country of his nationality or is able to return to the country of his former habitual residence (Art. 1.C CRSR);
- Persons who are at present receiving from organs or agencies of the UN other than UNHCR protection or assistance (Art. 1.D CRSR);
- A person who is recognized by the competent authorities of the country in which he has taken residence as having the rights and obligations which are attached to the possession of the nationality of that country (Art. 1.E CRSR);
- Any person with respect to whom there are serious reasons for considering that: (a) he has committed a crime against peace, a war crime, or a crime against humanity; (b) he has committed a serious non-political crime outside the country of refuge prior to his admission to that country as a refugee; or (c) he has been guilty of acts contrary to the purposes and principles of the UN (Art. 1.F CRSR).

b) Refugees versus Internally-Displaced Persons

Internally-displaced persons (**IDPs**) are individuals who have had to leave their homes due to persecution, but who are still within their countries of residence. Because they have never crossed an international border, they cannot be considered to be "refugees." Nonetheless, UNHCR has a mandate to work with internally-displaced persons. No treaty governs the protections to be afforded by internally-displaced persons, but some guidelines governing their treatment and protection exist.

C. Durable Solutions

Once an individual becomes a refugee, the international community, through the refugee regime, identifies a durable solution that ends the problems associated with displacement for the refugee and allows her to resume a normal life in a safe environment. There are three traditional durable solutions available for consideration: voluntary repatriation, local integration and resettlement.

1. Voluntary Repatriation

Voluntary repatriation involves the return of the refugee to the country of origin once the threat to freedom and safety has been eliminated. Repatriation must be a voluntary decision by the refugee. It is the responsibility of the international community to provide the refugee with clear and accurate information regarding the situation in their country of origin.

Given the current scale of the violence in Syria, and the probability that the conflict will continue in the coming years, voluntary repatriation does not appear to be a viable solution to the Syrian refugee conflict. Nonetheless, there are a number of refugees who opt to voluntarily return to Syria after having fled from the country. However, such repatriation is not due to the restoration of safety in Syria, but rather, to miserable conditions in refugee camps or in urban centers as well as the poverty and disease that are often characteristic of refugee life.

2. Resettlement

Resettlement is a means by which several countries can share the responsibility of protecting refugees, rather than placing the entire burden on countries adjacent to refugee-producing nations, such as Turkey, Lebanon and Jordan. Among the countries with resettlement programs are Argentina, Australia, Benin, Brazil, Canada, Chile, Denmark, Finland, Ireland, Netherlands, Norway, Sweden, the United Kingdom and the United States. The resettlement programs move refugees from a host nation to a third nation where they are granted permanent residence.

According to Ghandi Al Bakkar of Save the Children International, approximately 5,000 refugees had been resettled as of April 2014, mostly to Germany. This of course represents a small portion (approximately one quarter of 1%) of the approximately 4.3 million registered refugees that have fled Syria to date. Since that time, more countries, mostly European nations led by Germany, have offered to resettle additional Syrian refugees, and the US as of early 2014 had been considering raising the number of refugees, resolving in 2015 to increase its resettlement program. However, all of these offers in the aggregate constitute only a negligible percentage of Syria's more than four million refugees.

3. Local Integration

The refugee framework's second durable solution is local integration, whereby a host nation adjacent to a refugee-producing country absorbs the refugee population into its own population. Local integration in the host nation remains one of the primary durable solutions, but host nations are under no obligation to absorb refugees. If they do, refugees are granted the full rights of foreign residents and are assimilated into the local community with access to jobs, education, health care and basic services. If host nations are unable or unwilling to integrate refugees into their societies, then the refugees normally wind up living in refugee camps or living illegally in urban centers until another durable solution becomes available.

D. Temporary Settlements for Refugees: Refugee Camps

Where no durable solution may be implemented, refugee camps become a significant component of the refugee regime by providing refugees with temporary housing. In the camps, refugees are identified and registered and wait for a "durable solution" to materialize. Humanitarian aid earmarked for refugees is distributed in the camps, which become a means of serving the refugees with educational services, health care, food, water and temporary shelter, all while maintaining control of the population until a long-term solution is identified.

Many refugees do not like the confinement of the camps and choose to move to the urban centers of the host nation. This presents many challenges, both for refugees and for the refugee administration. Urban refugees tend to move more often, making it difficult for refugee agency caseworkers to keep track of them. They are also vulnerable in urban settings because they may be mistaken by local authorities as illegal immigrants as opposed to refugees with a right to employment. Urban refugees often settle in areas with limited access to education, health services and low quality housing. They are often subject to hostility from urban residents who do not distinguish them from growing numbers of unwelcomed economic migrants.

Refugee camps such as this one in northern Jordan are born when the international community is unable to achieve a durable solution to a refugee crisis. Such camps are intended to provide temporary shelter to refugees, but some camps have been in existence for decades.

Part II. The Camps

Chapter 3. Lebanon

A. Overview

1. Syrian Refugees in Lebanon

With more than one million Syrian refugees, Lebanon has been forced to bear the brunt of the Syrian refugee crisis. Today, one in every five persons in Lebanon is a refugee. Lebanon's population is now close to previously-project levels for 2050. The scale of this influx has had an enormous strain and impact on Lebanese local services.[19]

As of July 6, 2015, UNHCR had registered 1,172,753 Syrian refugees in Lebanon. However, the actual number of Syrian refugees is much higher; on May 6, 2015, UNHCR temporarily suspended new registrations as per the Lebanese government's instructions and, accordingly, individuals awaiting to be registered are no longer included in official UNHCR headcounts. Moreover, UNHCR's estimates do not include refugees living in urban centers that have opted not to register. The actual number of Syrian refugees residing in Lebanon is thus estimated by many experts to significantly exceed UNHCR's 1,172,753 figure.

2. Impact of the Syrian Civil War on Children

According to research conducted in Lebanon and Jordan, Syrian refugee children face staggering degrees of isolation and insecurity. Those who are not forced to work to support their families are largely confined to their homes. One statistic showed that as many as 29 percent of respondents stated that they leave their home—normally a tent, improvised shelter or crowded apartment—once a week or less.[20]

A significant portion of children have been physically wounded. Many have witnessed bombings, killings and other atrocities that can leave them psychologically wounded. Others have personally experienced egregious crimes of war, forever compromising their innocence. Anxiety, depression and difficulty in trusting others typically haunt refugee children long after they flee from Syria.

---

[19] *Futures Under Threat: The impact of the education crisis on Syria's children*, Save the Children (London: 2014), p. 19.

[20] UNHCR, "The Future of Syria: Refugee Children in Crisis," UNHCR UN Refugee Agency, available at <https://www.flickr.com/photos/unhcr/albums/with/72157638177114305>.

Far too many children have been physically and psychologically wounded In the Syrian civil war. Hassan, who lost three fingers due to bomb shrapnel, is one of thousands of children who have been crippled or mutilated in the Syrian civil war.

A further consequence of the conflict is a generation of Syrian children growing up without a formal education. Many children that have lost one or both parents and have been thrown into the role of caregiver, working long hours to support their siblings and other family members. Today, more than half of all school-aged Syrian children in Lebanon are not in school, and some 200,000 school-aged Syrian refugee children in Lebanon are estimated to remain out of school by the end of 2015.[21] Of Syrian refugee households in Lebanon, 18% that were surveyed gave "no space" as one of the reasons their child was not enrolled in school.[22]

---

[21] *Id.*

[22] *Futures Under Threat: The impact of the education crisis on Syria's children*, Save the Children (London: 2014), p. 20.

The requirement for children to work to support their families, the cost of enrollment and the lack of space in schools are among the reasons refugees give for not enrolling their children in schools in Lebanon.

3. Geographic Layout of Refugees and Tented Settlements

Lebanon, which is not a State party to the CRSR, has not permitted UNHCR to set up refugee camps within the Lebanese territory. This policy led to the settlement of Syrians throughout the Lebanese territory rather than in formal refugee camps.

Syrian refugees have become a part of Lebanon's demographic landscape. All across Lebanon's urban and rural settings, Syrian refugees can be found. Most of them reside in Lebanon in either urban centers or in non-formal settlements referred to as "informal tented settlements." In addition, there has been talk of an experimental camp at the Syrian-Lebanese border.[23]

a) Urban Centers

Syrian refugees have integrated with local communities in about 1,700 locations countrywide. Many are either renting accommodations or staying with relatives. Among those in rented accommodations, a sizeable number are in UNRWA refugee camps, given lower costs of rent in comparison with competing properties outside of the camps. For many of these refugees, paying rent and making ends meet is a daily challenge, and they can be found as mendicants on the streets of urban Lebanon.

[23] Minister of Labor Sejaan Azzi, a member of the ministerial committee dealing with the question of Syrian refugees, stated that "the decision to set up camps for Syrian refugees was taken at a cabinet meeting held on May 23, 2014 … [W]e decided in the committee to begin implementing the decision. We will establish two camps as an experimental first step that will be expanded later." See, *e.g.*, Eva Shoufi, "Lebanon: Political consensus over establishment of formal Syrian refugee camps remains elusive," *AlAkhbar English* (13 Sept. 2014), available at <http://english.al-akhbar.com/node/21514> (last accessed 10 Apr. 2016). However, to date, there has been no progress in the development of such camps.

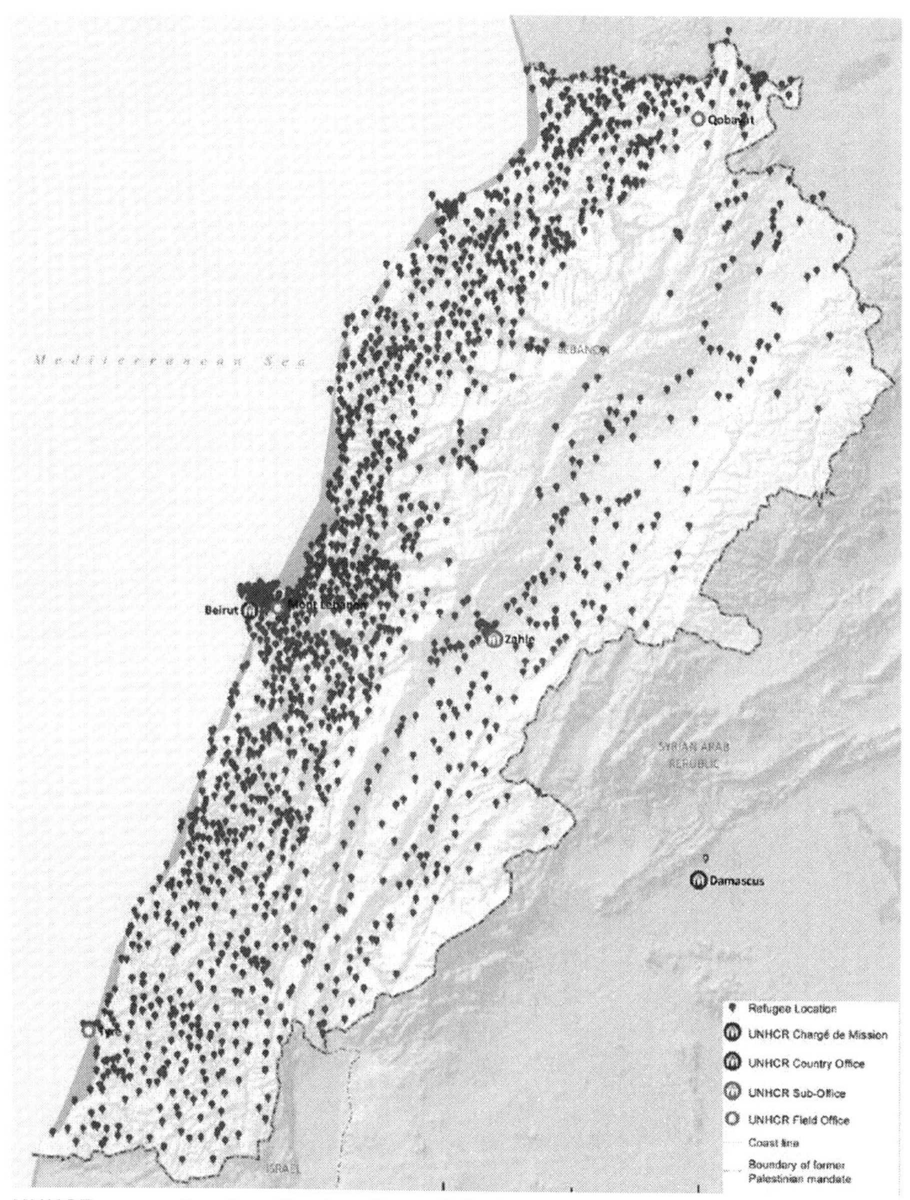

UNHCR map showing the location of Syrian refugees in Lebanon, with the greatest concentration being in and around Beirut.

b) Informal Tented Settlements

(1) Overview

Lebanon is divided into six governorates (*muḥāfiẓāt*, محافظات), as follows: Beirut Governorate, Nabatieh Governorate, Beqa‘ (Bekaa) Governorate,

North Governorate, Mount Lebanon Governorate and South Governorate. A sizeable portion of Syrian refugees[24] are currently living in the Eastern governorates, with most refugees having settled in Beqa', which lies on the Lebanese-Syrian border. Syrian refugees in Beqa' Governorate are concentrated into non-formal settlements referred to as "informal tented settlements" or "ITS."

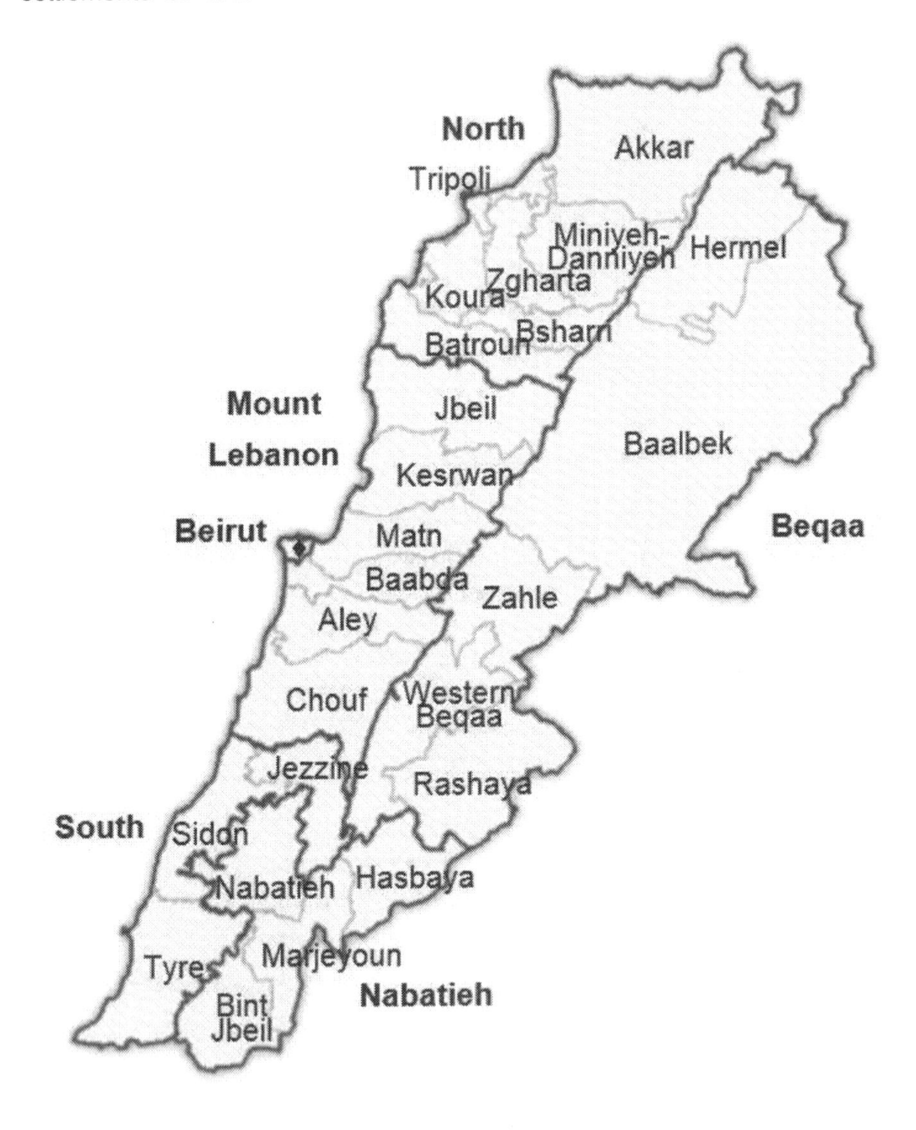

(2) Cost of Building and Maintaining Shelters

---

[24] Estimated by a source at the NRC at approximately 20%.

Unlike in formal refugee camps administered by UNHCR, refugees living in ITS must rely on their own financial resources to build and maintain their shelters. On the basis of conversations with households in the ITS, Norwegian Refugee Council Shelter Specialist Neil Brighton estimates that many refugees have invested approximately USD 1,400 over a period of time in building and maintaining their shelters. In addition to this expense, the vast majority of households are paying approximately USD 100 per month in rent. This expense covers merely the footprint of the shelter; in addition, the majority of refugees are required to pay approximately USD 40 per month for electricity. Further resources are required for water trucking.

A group of refugees erect a new shelter in Chtaura. The Norwegian Refugee Council estimates that Syrian refugees invest approximately USD 1,400 in building and maintaining their shelters in Lebanon.

4. Impact of the Syrian Refugee Crisis across Lebanon

The economic, political and security impact of the Syrian refugee crisis continues to deepen across Lebanon. The government has in response established an inter-ministerial crisis cell, confirming its pro-active engagement in refugee issues. Despite restrictions imposed at the border, it is expected that Lebanon will continue to provide Syrians in need of assistance and protection safe havens in Lebanon.

Refugees have access to most basic services through public institutions. However, despite this and the large-scale inter-agency response to date,

Syrian refugees are becoming increasingly vulnerable, especially as their savings are depleted.

In addition to more than 1.3 million Syrian refugees estimated to be residing in Lebanon, asylum-seekers from Iraq continue to make up the majority of new registrations among non-Syrians. Since June 2014, developments in Iraq, including the advance of the self-styled Islamic State of Iraq and Al-Sham (or Islamic State of Iraq and Syria) (**ISIS**), have led to a significant increase in registration requests.[25]

It is estimated that there are tens of thousands of stateless people in Lebanon, including Syrian refugees born in Lebanon. A 2014 survey of Syrian newborns found that nearly three quarters do not possess official birth certificates.[26]

5. Aid Agencies

Various aid agencies have set up humanitarian operations throughout Lebanon, both in Lebanon's urban centers, including Beirut and Tripoli, and field operations and the Beqa' Valley and beyond.

a) Norwegian Refugee Council

The Norwegian Refugee Council (**NRC**) has been present in Lebanon since 2006 and has been providing assistance to Syrian refugees since September 2011. Through its work and coordination with relevant stakeholders, NRC has identified a number of protection needs, including the necessity of information and legal counseling on the part of refugees fleeing Syria.

In Lebanon, the NRC coordinates a host of activities, including in the areas of water, sanitation and hygiene (**WASH**), camp management, education, awareness raising with respect to rights and access to services, counseling, legal assistance and representation before the Lebanon courts. Its programs are focused on both Syrian refugees as well as twice-displaced Palestinian refugees that previously resided in Syria and have been displaced to Lebanon since the beginning of the Syrian civil war.

Commencing in March 2012, the NRC Information, Counselling and Legal Assistance (**ICLA**) Programme in Lebanon has been providing assistance to refugees. The main ICLA beneficiaries have been Palestinian refugees already in Lebanon and refugees from Syria (including Lebanese returnees and Palestinian refugees from Syria). NRC seeks to provide these refugees with counseling and legal assistance in the areas of:

- the Lebanese legal system, including employment law for Syrian employees, municipal curfews and refugee rights under international and local law;

[25] UNHCR, "2015 UNHCR country operations profile – Lebanon," available at <http://www.unhcr.org/pages/49e486676.html>.

[26] UNHCR, "UNHCR Global Appeal 2015 Update," available at <http://www.unhcr.org/ga15/index.xml>.

- housing, land and property law, including on lease agreements and eviction;
- civil documentation, including the birth, marriage and divorce registration process; and
- the legal status of Syrian refugees and the issue of statelessness.

b) Amel Association International

Amel Association International provides health, hygiene and legal rights training to Syrian refugees in Lebanon. Through the European Union-funded project "Empowerment of Syrian Refugee Youth and Host Communities in Lebanon," Amel Association offers refugees aged between 15 and 30 years old with computer and vocational training and English-language instruction. Refugee youth are further given training and vocational opportunities in the form of internships. Those who experienced or witnessed war crimes are prepared to confront their traumas through psychological consultation and life skills training. Amel Association's partner organization ANERA offers refugee youth health, conflict resolution and communication trainings and tool kits. Amel Association further equips refugees with human rights tool kits to raise their awareness of the rights of refugees under international law.

Ghassan Ayash has worked in the humanitarian sphere for 36 years, since 1978. During the Lebanese civil war, he worked as an ambulance driver, where he took a bullet and was injured by flying shrapnel. He resumed his work as an ambulance driver after recovering from both injuries. At present, he works for Amel Association International, transporting trainees, refugees and supplies.

Among the Association's flagship programs, the EU-funded "Empowerment of Syrian refugee and host communities youths in Lebanon" seeks to contribute to the sustainable empowerment of Syrian refugee and host communities living in Lebanon by enhancing the professional capacities and life skills of refugee and host community youth. The program targets more than 4,250 direct beneficiaries who are all vulnerable youths affected by the Syrian crisis in Lebanon, including both host communities (Lebanese and Palestinian), Lebanese returnees and Syrian and Palestinian refugees. The program aims to empower these beneficiaries to improve their socio-economic conditions in Lebanon and to prepare Syrian refugees for reintegration into Syria when once they voluntarily decide to repatriate to their home country.

B. Legal Framework

1. Housing, Land and Property

Syrian refugees face specific protection and legal challenges linked to housing, land and property (**HLP**). These issues often result in a lack of tenure security for refugees in Lebanon.

As the number of refugees who must manage their own shelter situation is increasing, it is important to have an improved understanding of the circumstances leading to potential evictions. In particular, refugees who build their apartments or set up tents may be at high risk to be evicted if legal procedures, including building permit procedures, are not followed. This risk of eviction concerns refugees living in all types of housing situations, including private apartments or houses, informal settlements or in collective living situations on private or public land.

The main legislation regulating HLP in Lebanon is:

- Real Estate Ownership Law /3339/ L.R. dated 12 November 1930 (the **Real Estate Law**); and
- Legislative Decree Number 11614 dated 4 January 1969 and its subsequent amendments, notably Law No. 296/2001 (the **Foreign Ownership Law**)

The Real Estate Law defines buildings as building materials which are all collected and assembled together immovably whether on or in the ground (**Buildings)**. The Real Estate Law also defines real estate ownership as the right to use, enjoy and dispose of a property within the limits of the laws, decisions and regulations (**Real Estate Ownership**).

The Foreign Ownership Law provides that any non-Lebanese natural or legal person and any Lebanese legal person deemed by the Law as 'foreign' may not acquire by means of a contract or any other legal act between living persons any real estate right on the Lebanese lands or any other real estate right as determined by the Law, unless first obtaining a permit granted by Decree issued by the Council of Ministers upon the suggestion of the Minister of Finance. The only exception to this rule is in the circumstances explicitly prescribed for in the Foreign Ownership Law or in any other specific law.

C. Beirut's Urban Refugee Population

1. Overview

Syrian refugees have poured into Lebanon since 2011. Today, they can be found throughout urban centers, such as Beirut, and in rented apartments. Some are staying with family or friends. Many of Syria's poorer refugees, however, have been relegated to Beirut's Shatila Refugee camp in the Sabra neighborhood, which was originally established for Palestinian refugees in 1949, but since 2011 has swelled in population due to an influx of Syrian refugees.

Refugees are found in every corner of Lebanon's urban centers. Most of the refugees that one speaks with have come to Lebanon through a friend or other contact. Many are living in cramped quarters with several children crowded into a single room.

The economic standing of refugees living on their personal savings quickly takes a downward turn as their savings are depleted in Lebanon. Many struggle to pay rent or even feed themselves and their children. Some are dependent on the hospitality of friends or family, but the less fortunate ones are forced to fend for themselves, attempting to earn an income in Lebanon's uncertain low-wage jobs market. Others can be found throughout Beirut, begging on the streets, under bridges and near the entrances to hotels, all in the hope that a generous hand would be extended to them. Many children are forced to work to support their families, especially when one or both parents have been rendered incapacitated by the Syrian civil war. The requirement on refugee children to work further strains the already limited opportunities they have to pursue an education.

Refugee children throughout Lebanon's urban centers, such as these children in Beirut, are forced to work in order to help their families make ends meet. This is especially the case in families where the ability of one or both parents to seek work has become impaired by illness or injuries sustained In the civil war.

2. Societal Attitudes

Lebanon is a nation that has over the decades become accustomed to welcoming refugees. Since 1948, it has been the home of hundreds of thousands of Palestinian refugees and their progeny. Since 2011, Lebanon has hosted nearly one million Syrian refugees (over 1.3 million according to Lebanese government sources). The Lebanese have generously received their Syrian neighbors; 8% of all Lebanese households now comprise at least one Syrian refugee and 20% provide or have provided accommodations to Syrian refugees.

In contrast with this generosity, some attitudes in Lebanon have grown hostile towards Syrian refugees. Many of the Lebanese nationals interviewed in researching this book summarized Lebanese attitudes towards Syrian refugees as falling into one of the following camps: refugees are either viewed as threats to Lebanese security, as many refugees are former militants who contributed to Syria's present state of instability, or they are ordinary civilians that are putting pressure on Lebanon's infrastructure and limited resources. One of the main effects on Lebanon's economy is the impact that Syrian refugees have had on rental rates. As a result of the Syrian refugee crisis, all of the Lebanese are feeling the increase in rents that has resulted from the refugee influx and housing shortage. Many Lebanese also view Syrians as competing with them in Lebanon's limited job market. One national opinion poll confirmed that a majority of poll respondents considered Syrian refugees a threat to national security and stability and two thirds feared that the Syrian conflict would lead to civil war in Lebanon.[27]

Syrian refugees polled as part of this research confirmed these attitudes. Many complain about being looked down upon by their Lebanese "brothers." The cheap labor offered by Syrian refugees is often blamed for contributing to the unemployment of the Lebanese. Restaurants and small businesses set up by Syrians throughout urban centers in Lebanon are blamed for lost profits of competing Lebanese businesses. Furthermore, Syrians have been blamed by the Lebanese Minister of the Interior for a 50% increase in crime in Lebanon since the Syrian uprising began.[28]

3. Education

In October of 2015, UNHCR announced that Syrian refugees in Lebanon will be provided free education in Lebanese public schools up to grade nine. Beginning in 2015, the Ministry of Education and Higher Education, UN agencies and donors will pay all tuition fees, including the fees of USD 60 per child per year that even the Lebanese previously paid to enroll their children in public schools, and will further cover the costs associated with schoolbooks and stationary. International agencies that will cover these costs include UNHCR, UNICEF and the World Bank.[29]

This initiative aims to provide access to basic education to 200,000 Syrian refugee children between the ages of three and fourteen. UNHCR is particularly encouraging children who have been out of school for over a year as well as children with disabilities to enroll in the Lebanese school system.[30]

---

[27] Mona Christophersen, Jing Liu, Cathrine Moe Thorleifsson and Åge A. Tiltnes, "Lebanese attitudes towards Syrian refugees and the Syrian crisis: Results from a national opinion poll implemented 15–21 May, 2013," Fafo-paper 2013:13, ISSN 0804-5135, available at <http://www.fafo.no/images/pub/2013/10179.pdf>.

[28] Carine Torbey, "Syrian refugees in Lebanon fuel tensions," *BBC Arabic,* Beirut, 9 Apr. 2013, available at <http://www.bbc.com/news/world-middle-east-22029136> (last accessed 31 Aug. 2015).

[29] Nisreen Jaafar and Lisa Abou Khaled, "200,000 Syrian refugee children to get free schooling in Lebanon," UNHCR (Lebanon, 2 Oct. 2015), available at <http://www.unhcr.org/560e96b56.html>.

[30] *Id.*

New International School Kindergarten and Elementary School in the heart of Shatila Refugee Camp. Lebanon's Ministry of Education and Higher Education's initiative in partnership with international agencies seeks higher enrollment of both Lebanese and refugee children in the Lebanese school system.

At the same time, however, many struggling families face growing challenges in sending their children to school. Growing financial burdens are leading many Syrian children to forego formal schooling in Lebanon. Countless students have been forced to find work rather than attend school due to these financial burdens. At the time of this writing, Save the Children estimated that 80% of Syrian refugee children were out of school in Lebanon.[31]

4. Shatila Refugee Camp

a) Introduction

Shatila Refugee Camp, situated in southern Beirut, is just 10 kilometers away from Beirut's affluent Central District. The Camp has become an urban slum that contrasts the cosmopolitan seaside promenade of the Corniche a short taxi ride away.

The Camp is run by UNRWA for Palestinians refugees who fled or were expelled from Israel during the Arab-Israeli War. However, since 2011, thousands of Syrian refugees have made Shatila Refugee Camp their home. More than a third of the residents of the Camp surveyed identified themselves as Syrian.

b) The Refugees

(1) Overview

Most of the Syrian refugees of Shatila Refugee Camp are young families that fled Syria in the early years of the Syrian civil war. Many of the refugees surveyed had family that had already been living in Lebanon when they arrived, but in recent years, it has become more difficult for refugees to enter into Lebanon and settle into Beirut's urban areas.

(2) Profile of a Refugee: Abu Faris

Abu Faris came to Lebanon in 2011, in the early stages of the Syrian civil war when Syria's border with Lebanon was still relatively porous. His home in Homs, near the border with northern Lebanon, was ravaged early on in the war. Today, the entire neighborhood has been converted into military barracks.

Abu Faris's brother, already in Lebanon, arranged for Abu Faris to relocate to Beirut. Today, Abu Faris works in a scraps shop in the heart of Shatila Refugee Camp, living off of eager wages and struggling to provide for his wife and three children. UNHCR provides him with USD 60 per month and pays for his children's schooling, but the cost of food, shelter and utilities in Lebanon dwarf these allowances. Abu Faris applied to UNHCR to resettle to a third country, but he is on a long waiting list with thousands of other refugees. He still hopes that UNHCR will be able to arrange for him to live "anywhere in the world besides this refugee camp."

Abu Faris's entire family has fled from Homs. His older brother lives with him in Beirut. His sister escaped to the northern Syrian city of Latakia, making

---

[31] *Futures Under Threat: The impact of the education crisis on Syria's children*, Save the Children (London: 2014), p. 17.

her one of Syria's more than 7.6 million internally-displaced persons that have never crossed an international border. His half-brother fled to southern Turkey, eventually making his way up to Istanbul, where he currently lives.

Abu Faris in a scraps shop in the heart of Shatila Refugee Camp.

Abu Faris makes his living by selling scraps such as those pictured above.

c) *Housing*

(1) Concrete Buildings

Because Lebanon's refugee camps are prohibited by the Lebanese authorities from expanding outwards, Shatila is responding to its growing population and resulting increased demand for housing by expanding upwards, with story after story being added to block houses.

Multi-storied buildings such as this one are a typical site in Shatila Refugee Camp as buildings expand upward.

A new building erected in Shatila Refugee Camp is wrapped in a tangled web of wires and electric cables.

Typical block housing units of Shatila Refugee Camp.

Several local armed gangs have taken advantage of the camp's inaccessibility and countless narrow alleys and obscure passages to run black markets. Their presence often prevents international organizations from obtaining insurance to allow their workers to enter.

(2) Makeshift Shelters

As Syrian refugees have poured into Shatila Refugee Camp, they have improvised shelters in any open space they could find. Not having the resources to erect proper concrete buildings, they make due with extemporized homes made of whatever scraps they can collect. Often, these homes are constructed from wood scraps, sheet metal and plastic boards. Rags and blankets are often used as windows and doors.

Improvised shelters in the heart of Shatila Refugee Camp.

These homes are assembled through scrap wood and any other materials that can be collected by rummaging through garbage.

Makeshift shelters in the heart of Shatila Refugee Camp reflect a motley assortment of building materials.

These homes lack the durability to withstand rainstorms or to keep the living area free from rodents and other pests. They fail to insulate the living spaces during the winter or to promote a hygienic environment free from dirt, dust and debris.

D. Lebanon's Informal Tented Settlements

1. Introduction: The Refugees of the Beqa' (Bekaa) Valley

Many of Syria's poor refugees have found shelter in vast, informal tented settlement camps throughout Lebanon's Beqa' (Bekaa) Governorate, which lies on the eastern half of Lebanon, bordering Syria. Refugees have set up camps throughout the Governorate's five districts: Baalbek, Hermel, Rashaya, Western Beqa' (al-Beqaa al-Gharbi) and Zahle. Highly-populated unofficial groupings of Syrian refugees are located in the cities of Barr Elias, Arsal, Chtaura, Baalbek and El Ain.

Most of the tents that refugees erect are made of whatever scrap wood and other materials refugees manage to assemble. Refugees are especially challenged during winters, as many of their shelters lack proper insulation fall short of standards and indications for keeping out rain and moisture.

Two refugees about to tackle their second winter in Lebanon form part of the 55 percent of refugees estimated by UNHCR to live in sub-standard shelters, such as tents, garages, worksites and unfinished buildings. Credit: UNHCR/S.Hoibak

The eastern Governorate of Beqa' has become so overwhelmed by refugees that the Lebanese government in 2015 developed a plan to establish refugee camps at the Syrian-Lebanese border. The Cabinet had further decided to create residential compounds inside Syria or along the border for Syrian refugees.

UNHCR has issued a warning against this plan, given its experience that camps built in border areas can be transformed into hubs of armed activities. UNHCR further expressed concern over whether the Lebanese authorities could maintain security in remote border regions, many of which remain "lawless no-man's lands."[32]

---

[32] Elise Knutsen, "UNHCR opposes government plan for Syrian refugee camps," *UNHCR Refugees Daily* (2 June 2014), available at <http://www.unhcr.org/cgi-bin/texis/vtx/refdaily?pass=52fc6fbd5&id=538c0b758>.

Syrian refugees clear snow from the roofs of their tents in an ITS in the Beqa' Valley in early January 2015. To help mitigate the impact of Lebanon's freezing winters, UNHCR distributes plastic sheeting, wood and tools to help keep accommodations insulated. Credit: UNHCR/L. Abou Khaled

2. Barr Elias

a) *Overview*

The Barr Elias landscape is riddled with informal tented settlements. Improvised shelters hug city roads and coarsened tents dot the cityscape. Sixty to seventy thousand Syrian refugees have been said to live in Barr Elias alone, putting pressure on an already-fragile infrastructure.[33]

As an exception to these informal settlements, the Inma' (Inmaa) Compound, managed by the Lebanese organization Ighatheya, was developed in Barr Elias as an organized refugee settlement. The 30,000-square meter community has its own drainage system, clinic, school and water purifying plant. For some, the Inma' compound represents a new model for refugee settlements in Lebanon. Others, however, remain firmly opposed to building such compounds, citing their fear that Syrian refugees would never depart if given this level of support.[34]

---

[33] Elise Knutsen, "New model refugee camp set up in Bekaa Valley," *The Daily Star* (12 May 2015) available at <http://www.dailystar.com.lb/News/Lebanon-News/2015/May-12/297599-new-model-refugee-camp-set-up-in-bekaa-valley.ashx>.
[34] *Id.*

The mountains of the Beqa' Valley have largely become surrounded by refugees. Here, rows of tents fill a valley in Barr Elias.

b) Profile of a Refugee Family

Abu Haitham and his wife fled Aleppo, Syria, following clashes between government forces and non-state armed groups. They arrived to Lebanon with four children; since then, their youngest two were born in his refugee camp in Beqa‘.

Abu Haitham lost both of his legs following a bombardment of his apartment building. As the building collapsed around him, a falling wall crushed his legs. Both legs were later amputated, and prosthetic devices were affixed to enable him to walk. Even with the prosthetic devices, however, his mobility has been significantly compromised.

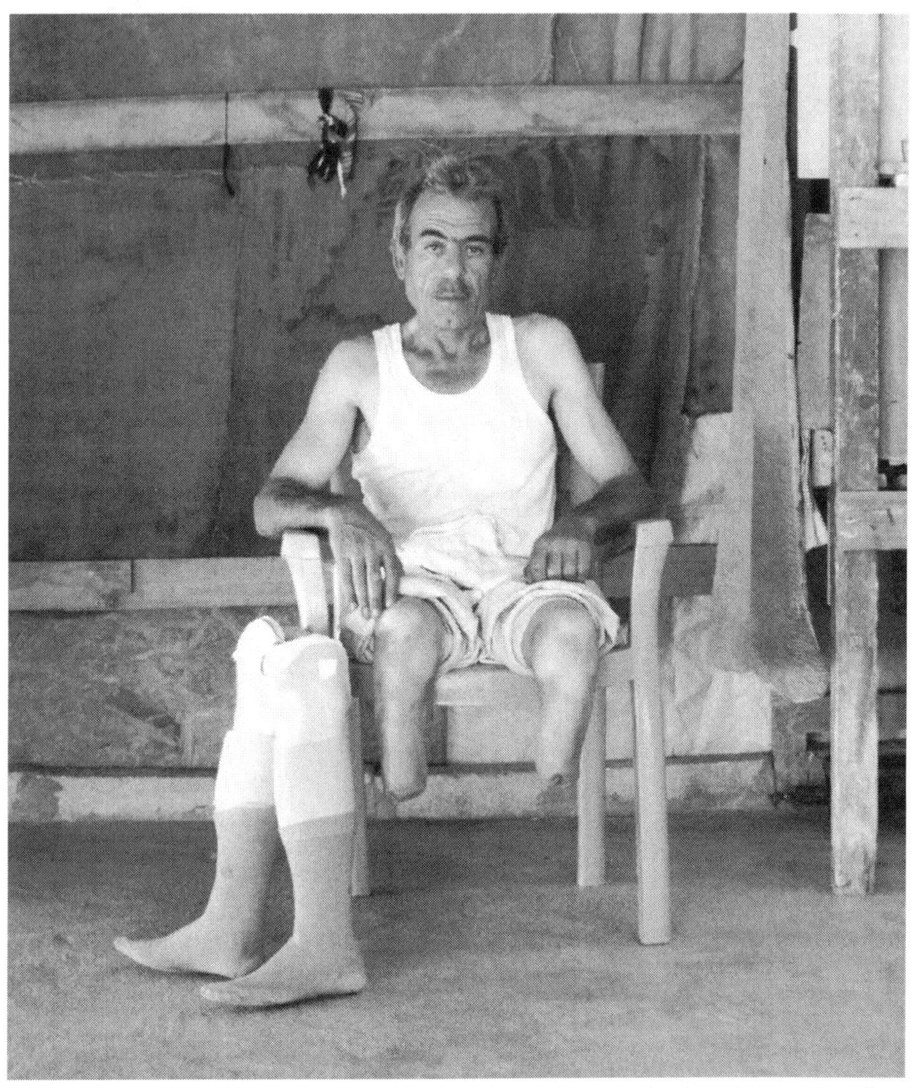

Abu Haitham's legs were amputated after they were crushed under a crumbling wall following a bombing in Aleppo. He poses next to two prosthetic devices that replaced his legs.

Abu Haitham is struggling to support a wife and six young children. UNHCR offers families in the Beqa' Valley USD 13.50 per month per family member, with a cap of five members per family. Abu Haitham thus receives the maximum capped allowance of USD 67.50 per month. This is enough to cover electricity, but little else.

His family is required to pay the owner of the land on which his tent is built LBP 100,000 (USD 66.67) per month (LBP 1.2 million (USD 800) per year) as rent. Electricity ranges from USD 40 to 60 per month.

Umm Haitham struggles to support six children with an allowance of USD 67.50 that she receives from UNHCR each month.

Their funds are insufficient for meat or vegetables; they live on a diet of bread and lentils. A barrel of clean water costs USD 7, but this water is often cloudy or discolored.

They are also unable to afford most medicines. When their youngest child fell ill in the summer of 2015, they were required by a hospital to pay a deposit of USD 400 as insurance over any fees that might arise as a result of treatment. Not having these funds, they declined medical treatment.

Abu Haitham's wife has applied to UNHCR for resettlement, but she believes the prospects of selection to be very low.

c) Housing Provided by UNHCR

For refugees arriving to the Beqa‘ Valley with special vulnerabilities, UNHCR provides special housing in buildings. These refugees are thus spared from living in the less stable and less durable tented settlements.

Muhammad and his son pose in front of the building informally known as the "UNHCR building" in Barr Elias. Muhammad's brother was in a compromised state of health after leaving a Syrian government prison. He is currently hospitalized in Beirut.

3. Chtaura

a) Overview

The large community of Syrian refugees in Chtaura is due in part to the fact that it is a transit town on the road from Beirut to Damascus. Moreover, the town is one of the first major populated districts on the road to Beirut. Today, throughout Chtaura, makeshift shelters line city roads, UNHCR canvasses can be found draping over buildings and coarsened tents dot the cityscape. Sixty to seventy thousand Syrian refugees have been said to live in Barr Elias alone, putting pressure on an already-fragile infrastructure.[35]

Improvised shelters hug every major road in Chtaura.

Many refugees complain that aid provided to them in Chtaura and in the Beqaʿ Valley generally is wholly unreliable. One grievance expressed by refugees is that aid workers, including UNHCR representatives, arrive to register refugees and occasionally provide them with assistance in the form of cash grants, but then disappear for long stretches at a time.[36]

---

[35] Elise Knutsen, "New model refugee camp set up in Bekaa Valley," *The Daily Star* (12 May 2015) available at <http://www.dailystar.com.lb/News/Lebanon-News/2015/May-12/297599-new-model-refugee-camp-set-up-in-bekaa-valley.ashx>.

[36] Claire Duffett, "With little aid in Lebanon, Syrians dig their own wells, forage for roofs," UNHCR Refugees Daily (4 Aug. 2013), available at <http://www.unhcr.org/cgi-bin/texis/vtx/refdaily?pass=52fc6fbd5&id=51ff3cef5>.

b) The Refugees

A Syrian refugee points to two barrels of discolored water. "We are forced to drink it," she says. "We have no other choice."

Su'ād, a widow with two sons, is in need of a cardiac catheterization that will cost about LBP 4 million (USD 2,667).

c) *Making a Living*

Refugees scrap together a living by selling fabrics and household items in the city center.

This impressive manor, stationed less than two kilometers from Chtaura's tented settlements, demonstrates the growing disparity between Syria's refugees and their Lebanese hosts.

Chapter 4. Jordan

A. Legal Framework

Since 2003, Jordan has hosted over 400,000 Iraqi refugees. Jordan was also a host for Iraqi refugees during the Gulf War in 1991 as well as Palestinian Refugees who fled the 1948 Arab-Israeli War, many of whom continue to live in refugee camps in Jordan today.

1. The Role of UNHCR

In 1998, Jordan signed a memorandum of understanding (hereafter MoU) with UNHCR, establishing the legal basis of the agency's presence in the country and the legal basis for refugee protections in Jordan. Jordan has not acceded to the UN Convention of 1951. However, the MoU does authorize registered asylum seekers to remain in Jordan for six months, during which time a durable solution must be found. UNHCR has been performing refugee status determination (**RSD**), a process which officially registers individuals as refugees with UNHCR and the government of Jordan.

Trailers such as this one can be found throughout temporary settlements managed by UNHCR.

2. Protection for Refugees

In 2003, Jordan issued a Temporary Protection Regime (TPR) to tolerate the presence of refugees in Jordan and prevent their deportation. The TPR was directed at any Iraqi refugee who could demonstrate arrival to Jordan in 2003 or later. Such refugees were permitted to remain for the duration of the TPR. Prior to the TPR, refugees who were registered with UNHCR under the MoU were entitled to six months of legal protection. However, since the signing of the TPR in April of 2003, most Iraqi refugees have not registered with UNHCR. Many of these unregistered refugees have bypassed UNHCR camps and have moved to the urban centers in Jordan. The challenge is that while unregistered Iraqi refugees are tolerated under the TPR, the Jordanian government officially considers their presence illegal without proper RSD and registration with UNHCR. Since 2005, the government of Jordan has notified UNHCR in writing that "it no longer considers the TPR regime as valid." Yet the presence of Iraqi refugees, registered or not, continues to be tolerated by the Jordanian authorities.

3. Durable Solutions

The Jordanian government does not consider local integration as a long-term solution for most refugees. Those with Jordanian spouses have been permitted to settle permanently in Jordan. Resettlement options to third countries have been limited since 2001 as nations with resettlement programs have heightened their security measures to prevent the spread of terrorism. While some measures of resettlement are still available, voluntary repatriation remains the most likely durable solution for refugees in Jordan. However, until the security in Syria and neighboring countries, including Iraq, improves and refugees living in Jordan are willing to return, they will remain in Jordan under the ambiguous condition of tolerated illegal refugees.

4. Refugee Settlement Conditions

Owing in large part to conditions in refugee camps where confinement and lack of freedom of movement have been described by some as a prison, the majority of refugees in Jordan have bypassed the formal refugee camps and settled in urban centers—principally Amman and Irbid. The settlement conditions of these refugees are difficult to quantify since these refugees fall outside of official refugee frameworks.

The presence of these refugees has placed a significant amount of strain on the infrastructure of urban centers. Many are unemployed and lack access to quality healthcare. Their children often do not attend school, but if they do, the schools are overcrowded because of the added burden of refugee enrolment. The presence of refugees has significantly increased the cost of rents, food, transportation and gas. This situation is very similar for both registered and unregistered refugees who have moved to the urban centers.

5. Partners in the Refugee Administrative System

The Jordanian Hashemite Charity Organization (**JHCO**) along with international NGOs, such as the NRC, works closely with UNHCR to support refugees both in camps and in urban centers. At Za'tari Refugee Camp, JHCO provides the management of the camp in close association with UNHCR.

A team of NRC aid workers take a break after a day of labor under the sun. NRC works closely with UNHCR and the Jordanian government in administering Za'tari Refugee Camp.

There have been significant attempts by the Jordanian government and by UNHCR to more efficiently administer the refugee regime. However, the absence of clear refugee legislation in Jordan coupled with overwhelming numbers of unregistered refugees settling in urban centers has placed an undue burden on Jordan's infrastructure, water and natural resources and the ability of the Jordanian government to properly address the social, health and educational needs of the refugees. A host of private charities and international NGOs have swept into Jordan over the past two years to contribute to the needs of the refugees, yet the international humanitarian community is largely overwhelmed by an influx of refugees that just a couple of years ago was never imagined.

B. Za'tari Refugee Camp

1. Introduction

Za'tari Refugee Camp in the Mafraq Governorate of northern Jordan, hosting approximately 80,000[37] Syrian refugees, currently stands as the fourth

[37] Syria Regional Refugee Response, Inter-agency Information Sharing Portal, Jordan, Mafraq Governorate, Zaatari Refugee Camp, "Total Persons of Concern," UNHCR –

Continued.../

most populous city in Jordan and among the largest refugee camps in the world, with some estimates ranking it as the world's second largest refugee camp. Unlike other refugee camps that compete in size, Za'tari Refugee Camp took only two and a half years to reach its current population. In contrast, Dadaab Refugee Camp in Northeast Kenya, which currently stands as the world's largest refugee camp, took two decades to reach its current size. If Za'tari Refugee Camp continues to grow at its current rate, it will soon surpass Dadaab and become the world's largest refugee camp.

Figure 2. Aerial view of Za'tari Refugee Camp. The desert landscape is characterized by unending rows of UNHCR tents and trailers.
Credit: US Department of State

2. Shelters

a) Arrival

Refugees entering Jordan must pass through customs and immigration just as any foreign visitor to Jordan. Since the bombing attack on a hotel in Amman in November, 2005, immigration authorities have tightened the restrictions for refugees seeking asylum and refugees are not always permitted to enter Jordan without proper documentation.

Once they cross through immigration, refugees will reach a refugee camp not far from the Jordanian border. In the case of Iraqi refugees fleeing the Second Persian Gulf War, they reached Ruwashed Camp near the border

---

The UN Refugee Agency, available at <http://data.unhcr.org/syrianrefugees/settlement.php?id=176®ion=77&country=107> (last accessed 10 Apr. 2015).

with Iraq. In the case of refugees fleeing the Syrian Civil war, they reach Za'tari Refugee Camp, just 7.5 miles (12 kilometers) from the Syrian border.

The northwest gate of Za'tari Refugee Camp administers the registration of newly-arriving refugees from Syria.

A Norwegian Refugee Council aid worker explains the intake procedure for newly-arriving refugees to Za'tari Refugee Camp.

Shelter where new arrivals to *Za'atari* Refugee Camp spend their first night.

Pavilion serving as an overflow shelter on evenings when *Za'tari* Refugee Camp experiences a surge in the refugee influx.

b) Tents

The UNHCR family tents, with a total area of 23 m^2 (16 m^2 main floor areas and two 3.5 m^2 vestibules), are suitable for families of five persons.

The standard tents used by UNHCR were developed by shelter specialists in close cooperation with UNHCR, the International Committee of the Red Cross (**ICRC**) and the International Federation of Red Cross and Red Crescent Societies (**IFRC**). The tents were designed to guarantee fitness for use in all climates, with an appropriate life span against the elements, at an affordable cost.

UNHCR publishes generic tent specifications that allow the tents to be manufactured by different suppliers around the world. This allows UNHCR to purchase tents wherever crises may arise, according to a competitive tender process. To participate in UNHCR tenders, manufacturers must first complete a validation process by qualifying a family tent sample in a UNHCR-approved laboratory. Even then, family tents are subject to continuous quality control.

UNHCR tents face extraordinary climatic challenges at Za'tari refugee camp, which experiences the full range of seasons and accompanying snow, storms and floods.

Tents are expected to be manufactured according to quality specifications that allow for a five-year shelf life under normal warehousing conditions. Once assembled, the tents must meet a minimal one-year life span, maintaining sheltering and waterproofing capacities in all types of climates. This is especially key for camps such as Za'tari, which, being based in harsh climates, are subject to the full range of climatic challenges, including snow storms, torrents, flooding, dust storms and blistering summers.

These residential trailers are the most coveted possession of Za'tari Refugee Camp, where residents are eager to upgrade from tents to these more durable units.

Despite their quality and specifications, the UNHCR tents have proven inadequate to meet the challenges of the Syrian refugee crisis. The tents were designed with a one-year life cycle in mind, but the Syrian civil war has already lasted over three years—much longer than anyone expected. At the same time, Za'tari Refugee Camp has begun taking on the appearance of a more permanent establishment with the installation of electrical poles and street lights and more refugees moving into residential trailers, which have been increasingly donated by Arabian Gulf countries. Of the 19,000 trailers that have been received, Oman has donated 3,500 and Saudi Arabia has donated another several hundred.[38]

3. Social and Economic Development

Kilian Kleinschmit, former UNHCR Head of the Mafraq Sub-Office and Za'atari Camp Manager, has been colloquially referred to as the "mayor" of Za'tari Refugee Camp. One of his priorities has been to move beyond the mere survival of the refugees and work towards their social and economic well-being and education. He seeks to achieve this through partnerships with

---

[38] *See* "Oman donates 3,500 trailers to Zaatari camp," *JordanTimes.com* (20 Jan. 2014), available at < http://jordantimes.com/oman-donates-3500-trailers-to-zaatari-camp> (last accessed 19 May 2014).

the private sector, smarter technologies and giving refugees opportunities to advance through training.

a) *Economy*

At the cross-roads of Africa, Asia and Europe, Damascus, the oldest continually-inhabited city, has traditionally been a center of trade. Entrepreneurialism and innovation are thus qualities ingrained in the Syrian spirit, and the displacement has brought an opportunity to develop this spirit. They bring this spirit with them to Za'tari Refugee Camp, where savvy Syrian entrepreneurs operate 3,000 shops with 10,000,000 € circulated on a monthly basis. At Za'tari, one can find much more than relief goods for sale. A stroll into the marketplace reveals a plethora of stores selling toys, pets, ice cream, cheese, *shawarma*, wedding dresses, perfume, shoes, lingerie, cleaning supplies, rugs ... the list goes on.

A refugee stands next to his ice cream machine and a tower of multi-colored ice cream cones.

A plethora of shops selling everything from desserts to toys, pets and perfumes line Za'tari Refugee Camp's main commercial street, colloquially known as the "*Champs-Élysées.*" Here, refugees can find relief against the hot desert sun with one of these iced orange, lemon or raspberry slushies.

A shop-owner prepares a rotisserie chicken package for two refugee children.

On the left, an agent distributes Orange® telephone SIM cards. On the right, used furniture, fans and other electronic appliances are sold.

This shop owner manufactures mattresses aimed at making the lives of refugees more bearable.

"Zaghloul's Arabic Smokes" sells wholesale and retail tobacco, cigarettes and *shisha*.

One finds no limit to Syrians' entrepreneurial spirit at Za'tari Refugee Camp. Here, a young boy walks out of a trailer that has been transformed into a barbershop. The sign reads "Zaid's Men's Barbershop."

There is no shortage of demand for Za'tari's thriving businesses. Besides the 3,000 humanitarian workers visiting the Camp on a daily basis, there is no shortage of Camp residents with funds to spend. Many come bringing their life savings or access their funds through the *Hawala* System (the "Western Union" of the Arab world). Then there are Syrians whose husbands managed to make it to the Arabian Gulf, who earn money in various services sectors and transfer funds to their families living in the Camp. And of course, there are the entrepreneurial Syrians doing business by phone, acting as agents in international sales, mediators in construction deals or wholesalers of Pakistani, Turkish or Sudanese products to destinations such as Doha, Dammam and Dubai.

The thriving food business of Za'tari Refugee Camp caters not only to the local refugee population, but also to the 3,000 aid workers who visit the Camp on a daily basis. Here, a man prepares a traditional Syrian dish for takeaway. The sign reads "*Shaqf kebab* grilled on charcoal." Behind him is a grocer.

Asayel Al-Sham Gallery displays wedding dresses for sale and for rent.

A wedding dress gallery display.

Technically speaking, these shops, operated by Syrians and set up as joint ventures with Jordanian partners, are illegal, since Syrians living at Za‘tari have neither residency cards nor work permits. Operating and managing shops therefore contravenes Jordanian law. However, not all of the workers are illegal. Safeway and Tazweed have been established in Za‘tari through joint ventures between Syrian refugees and local Jordanians who obtain work permits for their Syrian partners. However, the majority of other improvised shops and businesses are operated illegally, with neither government business licenses nor work permits for the Syrians operating the shops.

In any case, legal restrictions do not hold much sway over Syrians at Za'tari Refugee Camp, where 75 percent of Camp residences have private toilets—contrary to Camp regulations—and the same percentage of residences illegally tap into public street lights for electricity, creating an informal—and illegal—energy market.

b) Innovation

(1) Job Creation for Syrian Refugees

(a) Cash-for-Work

Through Save the Children, 400 Syrian refugees participate in the three tiers of the "Cash-for-Work" program: (i) teachers in the Za'tari schools; (ii) skilled laborers; and (iii) unskilled laborers (*e.g.*, as security guards in 45 locations), the goal of which is to give Syrian refugees ownership of the Camp.

(b) Cash Workers

A similar program is administered by the Agency for Technical Cooperation and Development (**ACTED**), a Paris-based, privately-owned, NGO established in 1993. Through its Cash Workers program, ACTED employs a large force of Syrian refugees that collect trash from the approximately 700 garbage bins distributed throughout the Camp.

(2) Upgrading the Homes of Jordanians to House Refugees

Another innovation has come in the area of urban housing for refugees. Traditionally in Jordan and in the wider Middle East, as families expand, so too do their homes, with new floors or other extensions added to the original structure. In Jordan, the Norwegian Refugee Council (**NRC**) has developed a proposal to benefit both home owners and refugees that have migrated to urban centers: Rather than pay an unending stream of rent on thousands of homes in Amman and other urban centers, the International Rescue Committee (**IRC**) has paid families to upgrade their homes with annexes to allow Syrian refugee families to live rent-free. The arrangement provides a three-way benefit: (i) families obtain a significant improvement to their home, which they will keep when refugees repatriate after the end of the war; (ii) Norwegian Refugee Council and other humanitarian organizations pay a single, up-front cost, rather than indefinite rental payments under the "Cash-for-Rent" program, which have the effect of raising rents and making housing unaffordable; (iii) refugees obtain a living space that, while annexed to a larger home, provides them privacy and at the same time, access to urban centers.

(3) Food Vouchers and e-Food Vouchers

The World Food Programme (**WFP**) initially distributed dry foods, but given complaints across the Camp as to the need for more variety, fruits and vegetables, has transitioned towards a voucher-based system of food distribution. The WFP now gives out vouchers of JD 10 per person per 15 days, or JD 20 per month. Refugees thus enjoy the ability to exercise choices they did not have previously by going to any one of the 16 Za'tari shops or two supermarkets and choosing for themselves what foods to purchase.

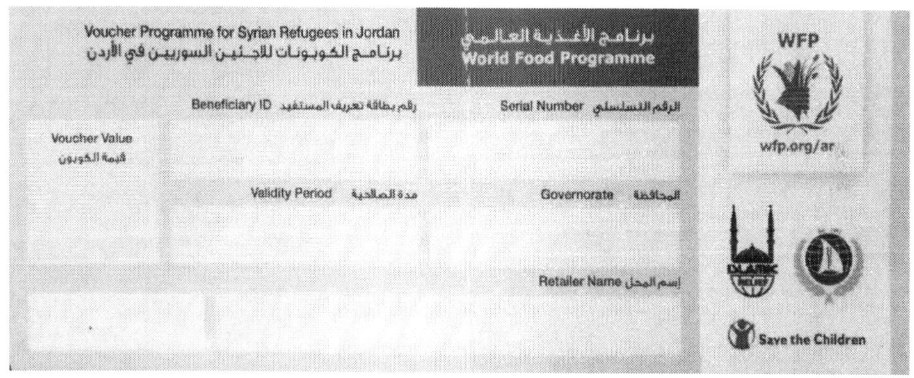
Voucher Programme for Syrian Refugees in Jordan
برنامج الكوبونات للاجئين السوريين في الأردن
برنامج الأغذية العالمي
World Food Programme
WFP
wfp.org/ar
Beneficiary ID رقم بطاقة تعريف المستفيد
Serial Number الرقم التسلسلي
Voucher Value
قيمة الكوبون
Validity Period مدة الصلاحية
Governorate المحافظة
Retailer Name إسم المحل
Save the Children

Sample WFP voucher provided two per month to Za'tari refugees. The logos of supporting organizations Islamic Relief, the Human Relief Foundation and Save the Children are printed on the vouchers.

The WFP will eventually completely phase-out the paper voucher program and replace it with an e-voucher program—essentially a credit card with the JD 10 pre-loaded on it by a Jordanian bank (most likely Al Ahli Bank) in a public-private partnership with the WFP.

c) Healthcare

A wide range of international medical and healthcare NGOs and international organizations currently operate at Za'tari Refugee Camp, providing everything from pro bono surgeries and other medical interventions to building education and awareness on personal hygiene, disease prevention and personal care. These organizations include Italian and Moroccan field hospitals and the International Organization for Migration (**IOM**), which offers screening of Za'tari patients and health relations with Jordanian Hospitals and the Jordanian Ministry of Health for treatment and a French military field hospital with a surgical unit specialized in treating war injuries. Other on-the-field organizations include:

- *Médecins du Monde* (Doctors of the World), which runs a primary healthcare center;

- *Médecins Sans Frontières* (**MSF**) (Doctors Without Borders), which offers refugees a wide-range of pro bono health clinics;
- Jordan Health Aid Society, which operates an ambulance corps and supports an emergency healthcare center;
- International Committee of the Red Cross (**ICRC**) and various National Red Cross and Red Crescent Societies, including the Jordanian and United Arab Emirates Red Crescent Societies;
- The International Medical Corps, which in partnership with UNHCR, the United Nations Population Fund (**UNFPA**) and the Jordan Health Aid Society, runs a comprehensive medical clinic for emergencies;
- The Institute for Family Health of the Noor Al-Hussein Foundation, which partners with UNHCR and UNFPA in providing health care; and
- UNFPA operates a reproductive health care unit and a primary health care clinic.

Gate of the *Médecins du Monde* Primary Health Care Centre, which provides refugees free medical consultations.

A Jordan Health Aid Society ambulance parked outside of a clinic and ready for deployment within the Camp.

The outer sign of a Saudi-funded health clinic. The sign reads: "Saudi Arabia-Kingdom of Humanity – The Saudi Campaign to Support the Syrian Brothers –Saudi Specialized Clinics at Za'tari Refugee Camp."

A refugee and his son stand outside a comprehensive medical clinic for emergencies that is administered by the International Medical Corps in partnership with UNHCR, UNFPA and the Jordan Health Aid Society.

d) Water and Sanitation

Even before Syrian refugees began streaming in, Jordan suffered from scarce water supplies. Public institutions often lacked sufficient water to maintain sanitation standards. Water supplies were often inadequate to perform the Islamic daily ablutions. Neighbors would often visit one another to obtain water, but would often find that their neighbors' water supply similarly ran dry.

At the inception of the Syrian civil war, the tense water situation further worsened. The thousands of refugees that poured in from Syria added stress to and increased tensions over the Jordanian water supply. Today, areas of Jordan with significant refugee populations face water shortages on the threshold of emergency levels.

Within this context, several international NGOs and governments have deployed to Jordan to help mitigate these concerns by implementing projects to meet the immediate needs of Syrian refugees, assuage tensions over scarce resources and improve water infrastructure. These organizations include:

- MercyCorps, which is digging new wells, upgrading city infrastructure and helping families install rainwater catchments and greywater treatment systems;
- German Federal Agency for Technical Relief (Bundesanstalt Technisches Hilfswerk); and
- Swedish Civil Contingencies Agency (**MSB**)

The MercyCorps trailer at Za'tari base camp displays a guide on proper hand-washing. MercyCorps' mission at Za'tari includes improving water infrastructure to better serve the Syrian refugee population.

e) *Law, Order and Criminal Justice*

One of the challenges that the Camp faces is crime. Refugees are reluctant to report theft and other crimes to the police because of an inherent distrust of authority. Kilian Kleinschmidt, who was brought to Za'tari in March 2013 to bring order to the camp, has stressed traditional mechanisms to fighting crime, such as isolating crooks and supporting local leaders who stand for community rather than crime and intimidation.

Still, outbreaks of violence, riots and assaults on humanitarian workers continue. In these cases, Jordanian criminal law applies, whether refugees are inside or outside of the Za'tari fence. While the Camp has its own set of internal rules and regulations, any act classified as criminal under Jordanian law—including, among others, theft, assault, rape and battery—may be prosecuted within the courts of Jordan. It is generally the Courts of the Mafraq Governorate that have jurisdiction to hear criminal cases brought against the Za'tari refugees.

UNHCR mobilizes a network of community volunteers to reduce, monitor and report crime. The agency depends on traditional community leaders, including *mokhtars* and *sheikhs* to mediate their way to peacefully resolving disputes and interpersonal conflict. When this does not work, 800 Jordanian police officers stand guard to ensure law and order and, where necessary, transfer violators of Jordanian law to the courts for prosecution. In addition to the Jordanian legal system, an informal network of local Syrian "religious courts" handle marriages, divorces and other changes to personal status, which in Syria have traditionally been subject to the institutions and traditions of the religion of the concerned individual.

A Jordanian non-governmental legal aid organization also works in training Syrian lawyers and establishing justice procedures at the Camp, as well as training protection officers.

4. The Humanitarian Community

a) *Overview*

Za'tari Refugee Camp demonstrates the way a diverse cross-sector of UN agencies work in tandem with governmental (*i.e.*, Jordanian) organizations and NGOs alike to provide humanitarian relief to Syrian refugees. One finds a wide range of organizations operating at Za'tari Refugee Camp, from organizations based in Japan to the Arabian Gulf to North America and beyond. To discuss the activities of all of the organizations engaged in Za'tari would fill many volumes. We thus focus on a representative sample of two UN agencies—UNHCR and the WFP, two NGOs—the Norwegian Refugee Council and Save the Children, and two faith-based organizations—World Vision and the Arab Center for Consulting and Training Services—each further discussed below in order to obtain a general understanding of the on-the-ground engagement of UN agencies and NGOs.

Japan Emergency NGO (JEN) is one of the countless international NGOs operating at Za'tari Refugee Camp.

b) United Nations Agencies

(1) United Nations High Commissioner for Refugees

As discussed earlier, the Office of the UN High Commissioner for Refugees (**UNHCR**) was established in 1950 to secure the fundamental human rights of the thousands of refugees displaced after World War II. Headquartered in Geneva, Switzerland, the agency is mandated with the task of supervising international conventions providing for the protection of refugees. The main principle behind UNHCR and refugee law in general is to provide surrogate international protection for an individual where national protection of his fundamental rights has failed.

UNHCR trailer at base camp displays the logo of UK aid, one of its sponsoring agencies.

At Za'tari Refugee Camp, UNHCR is the lead international organization responsible for administration. The Jordanian government agencies that work with UNHCR in implementation include the Public Security Directorate and the Ministries of the Interior; Planning and International Cooperation; Education; Health; Social Development; and Public Works and Housing. Jordan's National Centre for Security and Crisis Management is also active as a UNHCR operational partner.

(2) World Food Programme

The World Food Programme (**WFP**) is a UN General Assembly subsidiary organ headquartered in Rome that provides food assistance to address hunger and promotes food security. The WFP provides food to an average of 90 million people per year, the majority of whom are children.

The WFP focuses on distributing the kinds of foods that would be eaten by refugees back home. In the case of Za'tari Refugee Camp and Camps that host Arabs generally, food is an important staple diet food. The WFP therefore distributes fresh-baked bread every morning at the Camp in four sites from 6:00 am – 8:30 am daily, as well as biscuits to 12,000 children in three schools. The nutritional value of these foods is reinforced with fortified vitamins. In addition to food distribution, the WFP distributes vouchers to refugees for use throughout the Camp. The distribution of food and vouchers is executed mainly by Save the Children, the WFP's partner organization.

Upon arrival to *Za'tari* Refugee Camp, refugees receive their first meal package consisting of *ful mudammas* (a Syrian dish made from mashed fava beans and oil), hummus, crackers, tuna and a water bottle. Wherever in the world it distributes meals, the World Food Programme serves food that resembles refugees' diets in their home countries.

c) Non-Governmental Organizations

(1) Norwegian Refugee Council

(a) Overview

The Norwegian Refugee Council (**NRC**) is a non-governmental organization that promotes and protects the rights of refugees and internally-displaced persons who have fled their homes as a result of conflict, human rights violations, acute violence and natural disasters, among other causes.

The Norwegian Refugee Council focuses on five core activities:

- Shelter: emergency shelter, housing, schools and establishment of other forms of public infrastructure;
- Food Security: distribution of food and non-food relief items;
- Information, counseling and legal assistance (**ICLA**): focusing on housing, land and property, legal identity, statelessness and refugee status procedures;
- Water, sanitation and hygiene: access to clean drinking water, sanitation and waste management facilities; and
- Education: programs targeting children and youth.

It is funded by several international donors, with the Norwegian Ministry of Foreign Affairs, UNHCR, the Directorate-General for Humanitarian Aid and Civil Protection of the European Commission (**DG ECHO**) and the Swedish International Development Agency (**SIDA**) being its largest donors.

Other donors include:

- The Australian Agency for International Development
- Canadian International Development Agency
- Common Humanitarian fund
- Central Emergency Response Fund
- Danish International Development Agency
- Department for International Development
- Dubai Cares (a philanthropic organization working to provide education to children in developing countries)
- European Commission
- Food Agriculture Organization
- The Japan International Cooperation Agency
- The Khalifa Bin Zayed Al Nahyan Foundation
- Norwegian Agency for Development Cooperation (**NORAD**)
- Office for the Coordination of Humanitarian Affairs (**OCHA**)
- Refugee Education Trust
- Swiss Agency for Development and Cooperation (**SDC**)
- Stichting Vlüchteling
- United Nations Education, Science and Cultural Org. (**UNESCO**)
- UNICEF
- United States Agency International Development (**USAID**)
- The WFP

(b) Activities at Za'tari Refugee Camp

The Norwegian Refugee Council in many ways acts as UNHCR's on-the-ground implementing body at Za'tari Refugee Camp, distributing, pitching and making repairs to tents with about 250 "Cash-for-Work" Syrian refugee laborers and engaging in other UNHCR-outsourced activities. At the Camp, the NRC manages the area that each day receives newly-arriving refugees, which as of the time of this writing averages roughly five to six hundred refugees per day.

(c) ICLA: Providing Legal Assistance to Refugees

(i) Overview

NRC does not limit itself to assisting Syrian refugees at Za'tari Refugee Camp; rather, it provides key services to the thousands of refugees that have migrated to Jordanian urban centers, such as Irbid and Amman. One of the key services that it provides to these refugees is legal assistance in the field of housing. For example, with the launch of a new program to upgrade the homes of Jordanian families to be able to host Syrian refugee families (see "Upgrading Homes to House Refugees," above), many legal questions remain as to title and refugees' rights. Can a Jordanian family, after accepting the upgrade provided by NRC, then proceed to evict the Syrian refugee family and then take possession of the annex without providing the rent-free housing? What are the rights under Jordanian law if the locks are changed? This and other questions must be clarified in legally-binding and enforceable contracts and regular follow-up is necessary with the host families to ensure the protection of the rights of Syrian refugees.

(ii) Operation

At present, in part due to the fact that NRC does not yet know the scale of local needs, it works through local partners rather than through a large legal staff. Among these partners are the World Bank-funded Justice Center for Legal Aid (**JCLA**), which is trying to model a government-run legal justice system, and Arab Renaissance for Democracy and Development – Legal Aid (**ARDD-LA**), a Jordanian NGO that is UNHCR's partner for legal assistance. Run by Palestinian sisters, ARDD-LA trains Syrian lawyers in gathering information for human rights reporting and building capacity to support the bar that will one day return to Syria.

(iii) Focus Areas

ICLA focuses on the following areas of legal assistance in support of the Syrian refugees:

- Legal identity (*e.g.*, birth, marriage, death, etc.);
- Status and registration (*e.g.*, explaining the benefits of registering with UNHCR);
- Housing, land and property rights (*e.g.*, access to property in Jordan or to Syria upon return; Jordanian landlord-tenant law).

Among its activities, ICLA applies pressure to ensure displaced persons are able to return to their property and areas of origin. The UN Principles for Housing and Property Restitution for Refugees and internally-displaced persons (*i.e.*, the Pinheiro Principles) provides guidance on the management of the technical and legal aspects of housing, land and property restitution rights, which are of key importance to refugees and internally-displaced persons. A key concern is to prevent third parties from benefitting from conflict and seizing control of property. A second concern is to ensure the respect of the property rights of refugees and internally-displaced persons, particularly in situations where ownership becomes ambiguous under local law, such as in cases where the death of an original owner may leave dependents without a clear claim to the land.

(2) Save the Children

(a) Overview

Save the Children International is an independent non-governmental organization established in the United Kingdom in 1919 that promotes children's rights and supports children in developing countries. Fully funded by individual contributions, the organization aims to improve the lives of children through better education, health care, and economic opportunities, as well as providing emergency aid in natural disasters, war, and other conflicts. While Save the Children almost exclusively focuses on Syrian children at the present, it has in the past worked with other vulnerable groups, including Iraqi refugees that fled to Jordan following the 1990-91 and 2003 invasions.

Save the Children has had a Jordan country office since 1984 and is the largest agency on the ground in Za'tari, with 350 Jordanian staff and 400 Syrian refugees volunteering in the "Cash-for-Work" program. The organization runs three kindergartens with 1,200 children as well as two multi-activity centers for youth between 15 and 25 years old, gyms and sports facilities. Save the Children also runs one-month "catch-up lessons" in areas such as Arabic, French, English, religion, etc., consisting of twelve lessons of 1.5 hours each, where a refugee who is otherwise illiterate might, for example, learn to write his or her name.

(b) Public-Private Partnerships and Volunteer Opportunities

Save the Children has welcomed some volunteers, most notably from Japan for six-month intervals and runs public-private partnerships with community-based organizations outside of the Camp that target Jordanian and Syrian refugees.

d) Faith-Based Organizations

(1) Overview

Faith-based organizations, including churches, mosques and faith-based international organizations such as World Vision, similarly work to fundraise on behalf of and provide relief to refugees.

(2) Arab Center for Consulting and Training Services

The Arab Center for Consulting and Training Services is one such organization. The Center works with refugee populations that require the most help, namely, the Syrian refugees who have just arrived and have not yet been registered with the UN, which can take 3-6 months. They provide 1,000 parcels of food every month and 1,000 non-food items every 6 months. They distribute in Irbid, northern Jordan, which hosts many refugees who do not live in camps. Rather, they rent apartments, sometimes with as many as 10 to a room. Whenever these individuals are accepted into the UN system, the Arab Center stops providing assistance since they target only individuals with the most need.

They also work with post-trauma counseling and train 700 women that they meet with regularly. Many of these women experienced violence before their eyes, sometimes seeing their husbands or even children killed. The Center seeks through counseling to help these women to overcome fears and anger, treat them with love and restore their human dignity.

In addition to international agencies and NGOs with a formal, registered presence at Za'tari Refugee Camp, countless charitable agencies, private companies and faith-based organizations visit the Camp to explore partnerships and deliver various forms of aid. Here, a representative from a faith-based organization in Mexico poses with Syrian refugees during a field visit.

5. The Refugees

a) *Social and Political Inclinations*

Most of the refugees living at Za'tari Refugee Camp are natives of villages and cities of southern Syria, the most prominent of these being Dar'a, which ignited the civil war when 15 children were arrested for painting anti-regime graffiti on a school wall. The refugees tend to be conservative *Sunni* Muslims that oppose the government of President Bashar Al-Assad. Many refugees previously fought with the Free Syrian Army in order to overthrow Al-Assad and establish a regime with greater human rights protections and political freedom. Others fought with more radical groups that have sought to replace Al-Assad's secular government with a *Sunni* Islamic State. According to some reports, such groups continue to recruit among refugees, encouraging young adolescent males to join their cause.

These sisters reached Za'tari Refugee Camp from Dar'a. Most of the refugees are conservative *Sunni* Muslims.

Two girls on their way back from a Save the Children-sponsored school.

Traditional Islamic dress for women—including the black *abaya* (a long, flowing outer garment) and *hijab* (head covering), can be seen throughout Za'tari Refugee Camp. In more conservative families, the *niqab* (facial covering) is also worn.

More conservative families do not permit the interaction of adult females and unrelated males. These families tend to support a government that enacts laws more closely aligned with the *Shari'a* (Islamic law) rather than on secular codes, with some taking stricter interpretations than others.

Due to rebels' general support of the revolution, the three-starred Syrian rebel flag can be seen flying over tents, trailers and businesses throughout Za'tari Refugee Camp. The rebel flag is bought and sold in shops as keychains and decorations.

The three-starred flag of the Syrian National Coalition for Opposition and Revolutionary Forces flies above various businesses in Za'tari Refugee Camp's commercial district. The Arabic word for freedom is written above the three stars of the Syrian rebel flag. Below the stars, the same word appears in English.

Among hats, belts and other accessories sold in this shop on the Syrian *Champs-Élysées*, the three-starred rebel flag can be purchased in its full-size or as a decorative key chain.

While refugees for the most part continue to oppose Al-Assad, their enthusiasm for the opposition has waned as extremist groups such as ISIS have joined the effort to overthrow Al-Assad. These groups, including the Al-Qaeda-linked *Al-Nusra* Front, have not hidden their intention to replace Al-Assad's secular government with an Islamic State that severely restricts basic rights and freedoms. Another group of leading rebel groups in Syria announced in 2013 that they were joining a new Islamic Front comprised of *Ahrar al-Sham*, *Jaysh al-Islam*, *Suqour al-Sham*, *Liwa al-Tawhid*, *Liwa al-Haqq*, *Ansar al-Sham* and the *Kurdish Islamic Front*. The many crimes of extremist groups operating in Syria, including the kidnapping and execution of civilians and the torture and beheading of captured members of the Syrian Armed Forces—with one rebel leader having posted a video of himself cutting out and eating the heart of a fallen regime soldier—have caused many Syrians to reconsider their political alignment.

b) *Children and Education*

(1) Overview

Refugee children have suffered the most devastating effects of the civil war. Most of them have witnessed bombings, killings and other atrocities of war that can leave them psychologically traumatized. Having had their lives uprooted in their flight from war, refugee children often experience anxiety, depression, anger and difficulty in trusting others. Many have lost one or both parents and have been thrown into the role of caregiver. These children turn in their childhood and education to become breadwinners, working long hours to support their siblings or other family members.

UNICEF works in partnership with several aid organizations to address these issues, but they face a wide range of challenges, including getting children who have witnessed traumas to concentrate in a classroom setting and obtaining high levels of attendance when most families view the camp as a temporary settlement and do not wish to integrate by sending their children to school or building community. Thus, rather than spending their days in the classroom, many children can be founding working in the marketplace, buying and selling vegetables and other goods and helping to support their families.

Yet despite these and other issues discussed below, the children of Za'tari have not lost their spirit: Throughout the camp, they can be found running and playing all kinds of games improvised from the very little that they have at the Camp.

Children running with a makeshift rope at Za‘tari Refugee Camp.

Children at the Camp make the best of what little they have.

Siblings playing outside of their trailer.

After more than three years of war, children face poverty, malnutrition and a resurgence of diseases such as polio. Many of these children arrive to refugee camps with nothing more than the tattered clothes they are wearing. Infants who survive birth come into the world without access to basic provisions, such as baby milk. Those who have not been so fortunate to find work are often reduced to begging when no caregiver is available.

This child stands next to a pile of debris and makeshift piping outside of his trailer at Za'tari Refugee Camp. The lives of countless children such as this one have been reduced to poverty.

(2) Education

UNICEF acts as the lead educational agency at Za'tari Refugee Camp. It engages with a wide range of partners in implementing educational and training programs.

UNICEF trailer at base camp.

UNICEF partners that operate at Za'tari Refugee Camp include:

- Save the Children – Jordan, which is working to enroll children of Syrian refugees in the Camp in schools as a part of the educational outreach program and administers "catch-up lessons" in areas such as Arabic, French, English and religion, consisting of twelve lessons of 1.5 hours each, where a refugee who is otherwise illiterate might, for example, learn to write his or her name;
- The International Rescue Committee (**IRC**), which is active in assessing gender-based violence;
- The International Organization for Migration (**IOM**);
- The Norwegian Refugee Council (**NRC**), which provides informal education services;
- Relief International, which administers a remedial education center in the Camp providing classes in Arabic, Math, Science and English for grades one through eleven. The remedial classes enable the children to develop the skills that will help them succeed in the formal classroom setting;
- United Nations Population Fund (**UNFPA**).

The gate of the Relief International Remedial Educational Center, which is administered jointly with UNICEF to enable refugee children to develop the skills that will help them succeed in the formal classroom setting.

UNICEF building with the Arabic script "Remedial Educational Center" printed on its side.

One of the main issues the Camp faces is that of school attendance. Because many of the Camp residents do not see themselves as living at the Camp long-term, they have little incentive to integrate locally and send their children to school. Thus, out of a pool of approximately 38,000 children, only about 5,000 regularly attend school. The sense that most refugees have that their residence in the Camp is temporary impedes the growth of community in the Camp in general and at schools in particular.

Those who do attend school have complained of the quality of education. Teachers who may not have training in the psychological and social issues that these children face often handle classrooms with as many as 60 children. Other challenges include the mental state of children who may have witnessed bombings and massacres or who might be separated from their parents or brothers or sisters. Such traumas could exact a heavy psychological toll, making it difficult to concentrate in the classroom.

UNICEF / Save the Children trailer-tents provide educational workshops for refugee children.

(3) Child Labor

All throughout Za'tari Refugee Camp, children can be found in the marketplace, selling goods, pulling wagons, transporting products and so forth. They can be seen behind fruit stands, strolling by caravans offering juice and other refreshments, and even at the sight of new tents being pitched. Many of these children are supporting their younger brothers and sisters, and some have been separated from their families altogether.

Children guide a donkey through Za'tari's commercial district.

Children transport a wagon through a residential section of the Camp.

Often, when a family wishes to move their tent to another district or closer to family or friends, they will hire children who, for a modest sum, will move and re-pitch the tent.

A Syrian youth pulls a donkey through the marketplace.

c) *Profile of a Refugee: Abu Hussein*

Abu Hussein lived in Dar'a before the start of the Syrian uprising. He worked as a baker who had mastered the art of the popular Syrian *fataya*, a salty pastry that can be made with *za'tar* spices, yogurt, vegetables or cheese. He sided with the rebels when he heard of the Syrian regime's crackdown on demonstrators demanding greater political freedom, following the arrest of 15 children who were arrested in Dar'a.

In 2012, Abu Hussein joined the Free Syrian Army to attempt to overthrow the Assad regime. In the course of one battle, an explosion caused an injury that demanded the amputation of his left leg, after which he laid down his arms. In the ensuing months, the fighting grew in intensity, with Dar'a having been the center of the revolution for many months. Houses were leveled and Abu Hussein, like thousands of other Syrians, was an internally-displaced Syrian. He had six children and a wife to support, was largely disabled from the fighting and his house was in ruins.

Like millions of other children caught up in the Syrian civil war, Abu Hussein's children have suffered the most devastating effects of the war, having witnessed bombings and other atrocities and having had their lives uprooted in their flight from war.

In 2013, Abu Hussein's family crossed the southern Syrian desert to find refuge in Jordan. In some ways, they are lucky to all be alive and together; many Syrians suffer worse fates, with some children having been separated altogether from their families. Abu Hussein's trailer is one that is filled with hope and hospitality. The family has little more than the clothes that they wear and vouchers that the WFP provides to keep them nourished, but they show the same hospitality that Syrians are known for. Aid workers and other guests are offered coffee and juice and Abu Hussein shows great interest in his guests. There is a good deal of gratitude to the international community for providing for these refugees, but the overwhelming desire of Abu Hussein, as with most refugees, is to return to Syria and try to build a normal life.

Neighboring children visit Abu Hussein's trailer. Despite the horrors that many have witnessed, Syrian children can still be seen throughout the Camp, running, laughing and playing.

C. Jabal Al-Hussein Refugee Camp

1. Introduction to the Palestinian Refugee Framework

a) Overview

Up to this point, we have been discussing UNHCR. Yet a second refugee agency exists within the UN framework. Prior to the establishment of UNHCR, the United Nations Relief and Works Agency for Palestine Refugees in the Near East (**UNRWA**) was established by the General Assembly in 1949 to provide assistance and protection through relief and jobs to 652,000 Arabs who fled or were expelled from Israel during the Arab-Israeli War. Today, UNRWA provides assistance to some five million Palestinian refugees living in the West Bank, the Gaza Strip, Jordan, Lebanon and Syria to achieve their full potential in human development, pending a just and durable solution to their plight.

UNRWA's services encompass the following forms of assistance:

- health care;
- education;
- social services and job provision (in public works projects);
- camp infrastructure and improvement;
- microfinance; and
- emergency assistance

With over 32,000 staff, UNRWA is the largest UN organization. The overwhelming majority of UNRWA staff members (more than 30,000) are locally-filled by Palestinians, thus fulfilling the organization's mandate to provide jobs as well as relief services.

What first strikes the casual observer is the presence of permanent structures at the UNRWA camps, which replaced the tents that Palestinian refugees originally lived in with more durable shelters.

b) Mandate: Protection and Assistance until a Durable Solution is Available

UNRWA has a very narrow and distinct mandate when compared to UNHCR. Its mandate is to provide protection and assistance for Palestinian refugees, who are operationally defined by UNRWA as "persons whose normal place of residence was Palestine between June 1946 and May 1948, who lost their homes and livelihood as a result of the 1948 Arab-Israeli conflict." This definition also includes the decedents of those identified as Palestinian refugees.

Under UN GA Resolution 302 (IV), which established UNRWA, the only acceptable durable solution available to Palestinian refugees is repatriation. With some exceptions, Palestinian refugees thus have not always assimilated into their host nations. Rather, they have been born and live in refugee camps run by UNRWA, which provides education, health care and in many cases, jobs.

Under its mandate, UNRWA takes no position on durable solutions and is not mandated to deal with durable solutions. Its mandate is strictly to provide relief for Palestinian refugees until the Israel-Palestine conflict is settled.

c) *Challenges*

(1) Funding

Since UNRWA is funded almost entirely by voluntary contributions rather than by mandatory assessments, UNRWA must actively seek funding from donors. UNRWA has been consistently underfunded during the past decade and is eagerly seeking funding. The UNRWA private partnership unit (Partnerships Division) works to support the organization from a financial perspective.

(2) Caseload

In addition to the overburdened caseload that UNRWA is handling, the Syrian conflict presents a new set of challenges in working with Palestinian refugees in Syria: access, security of persons, basic necessities of life and the outflow of refugees from Syria into Lebanon, where 1 million refugees have entered a population of 4.5 million with a current caseload of 250,000 Palestinian refugees) and Jordan.

(3) Other Challenges

Other challenges to UNRWA's work include the foreign military occupation of the West Bank and forcible resettlement therein as well as the Gaza blockade.

2. Jabal Al-Hussein Refugee Camp for Palestinian Refugees (UNRWA)

a) *Overview*

Jabal Al-Hussein Refugee Camp for Palestinian Refugees in northwest Amman, Jordan, is one of four camps set up in Jordan to accommodate refugees who fled Palestine following the 1948 Arab-Israeli war. The Camp was established in 1952 for 8,000 refugees, replacing the original tents in which Palestinian refugees lived with more durable shelters, for which UNRWA provided roofing. The camp has since grown into an urban quarter, a mini-city within Amman.

Jabal Al-Hussein Refugee Camp replaced the original tents with more durable shelters, for which UNRWA provided roofing. This cityscape reflects the buildings that have been erected over half a century, forming a city within a city.

b) Population and Layout

Jabal el-Hussein Refugee Camp hosts over 29,000 registered refugees. This figure grew after the 2011 onset of the Syrian civil war, which triggered the exodus of thousands of Palestinian refugees that previously lived in UNRWA camps in Syria. Today, many Syrian Palestinian refugees—mostly unregistered—populate Jabal Al-Hussein Refugee Camp and other UNRWA camps in Jordan and Lebanon.

Like other camps in Jordan, Jabal el-Hussein Refugee Camp faces severe overcrowding. The only way to accommodate further shelter is to build upwards, and this is exactly what refugees have done, vertically expanding by adding stories above existing structures.

Stories are often haphazardly added to buildings. As a family expands, an extra level is often added to accommodate married couples and their children.

Refugee camp cityscape. Jabal Al-Hussein Refugee Camp's layout is marked by winding alleys weaving between buildings.

Children make their playgrounds between concrete blocks in narrow passages between buildings.

c) Camp Programs and Education

Among the programs run by the Refugee Camp, Jabal Al-Hussein hosts a food distribution center, a health center, a community-based rehabilitation center, a women's program center and four schools. These programs and centers focus on health, education, social safety-nets, relief and social services and community-based rehabilitation.

However, like many UN agencies, UNRWA is often unable to secure sufficient funding to meet its mandate. UNRWA has repeatedly held conferences warning donors of its precarious financial situation, which has led to reductions of services and humanitarian aid. Some UNRWA programs lack sufficient staff, and the Agency has in the past faced uncertainty as to whether it would be able to meet payroll. Many UNRWA schools face overcrowding and funding shortages the inability to complete construction projects and delays in much-needed infrastructure improvements to the Agency's ailing school buildings.

While not in school, children can be found playing in the alleys that wind through the Refugee Camp. Here, children compete in an improvised soccer match.

Syrian refugee children make their playground among discarded tires and broken bottles. Here, children play near a dumpster, clipping a wire hook to a mattress and "fishing" for garbage.

d) *Economic Cross Section of the Refugees*

Poverty and high unemployment rates are among the major problems faced by Camp refugees. According to the Middle East Monitor, 60 percent of

Palestinians in Jordanian refugee camps live below the poverty line, about 45 percent are unemployed and 75 percent do not possess property.[39] This is partially due to underfunding of UNRWA, which has in recent years been unable to raise sufficient funding to meet its program goals, and partially due to refugees' inability to generate sufficient income in order to provide for themselves and their families.

The majority of refugees support themselves through small businesses and individual proprietorships, such as grocery and hardware stores. Others work as day laborers, builders or contractors. Still others work as employees of UNRWA, which employs thousands of Palestinian refugee workers as teachers, social and healthcare workers and laborers. Most of UNRWA's more than 32,000 employees are Palestinian refugees, with only a small minority of employees being international expatriate staff.

Poverty among refugees is exacerbated by the policy of employing only Jordanians in the government, military, police and security sectors. This policy, known as "Jordanization," is designed to decrease unemployment rates among Jordanian refugees. Some refugees feel that the policy is due to doubts as to Palestinians' loyalty to the Jordanian State. Others complain that the policy is one of many manifestations of discrimination against them. To address this issue, King Abdullah initiated a process in 2003 called "Jordan first" to create guide lines for reforms. The issue of unity and discrimination was also discussed in the forum "We are all Jordan," which brought together 700 decision makers, journalists and academics to discuss ways to bring about unity in the country. Still, one finds vast socio-economic discrepancies between the Palestinian refugee camps and the rest of Jordan. The influx of Syrian refugees to the Jordanian camps has further exacerbated the problem as thousands more have crowded into camps, competing for jobs and limited resources.

---

[39] "Sixty percent of Palestinian refugees in Jordan camps live below the poverty line," *Middle East Monitor* (23 Aug. 2010), available at <https://www.middleeastmonitor.com/news/middle-east/1447-sixty-percent-of-palestinian-refugees-in-jordan-camps-live-below-the-poverty-line> (last accessed 6 June 2014).

Small, family-run businesses that pass down from generation to generation make up the bulk of the Palestinian economy. Here, the sons of Abu Aoud manage and run their father's glass and mirror shop.

A blacksmith cuts through iron bars in a Jabal Al-Hussein metal shop.

Grocery stores, falafel restaurants and stores selling everything from chalkboards to live chickens characterize the main avenue running through the heart of Jabal Al-Hussein Refugee Camp.

Two Syrian-Palestinian refugees stand at the entry of a Jabal Al-Hussein fabric shop. Refugees such as these have been twice or thrice displayed, first from Palestine to Syria and now from Syria to surrounding countries. Hassan, pictured on the right, reports that shelling has buried his home in rubble.

When income does not exceed rent, small businesses are abandoned. Here, "For Sale" is spray-painted on the entry gate of this establishment.

One of Jabal Al-Hussein Refugee Camp's many abandoned businesses.

Chapter 5. Iraq

A. Refugees and Internally-Displaced Persons of Iraqi Kurdistan

The advent of the self-proclaimed Islamic State of Iraq and Al-Sham (or Syria) (**ISIS**), has exponentially compounded the Syrian refugee crisis. ISIS's expansion across northern Iraq has led to the displacement of both Iraqi internally displaced persons (**IDPs**) and Syrian refugees in Iraq, thus rendering them twice-displaced. According to the World Bank, the refugee and IDP crises have imposed substantial strains on the social sectors of Iraqi Kurdistan and increase stress on the region's infrastructure, including its water, waste management, energy and transport sectors.[40]

ISIS's June 2014 conquest of Mosul triggered one of the greatest flows of Iraqi IDPs and Syrian refugees in northern Iraq. Following ISIS's occupation of Mosul, Christians, Yazidis, Shi'as and Sunni Kurds fled Iraq's Nineveh Governorate to Erbil Governorate to the East, and the Dohuk Governate to the North.

Today, the Kurdistan Region is hosting nearly two million refugees and internally-displaced persons. Most of these refugee camps and internally-displaced persons are concentrated in and around the Erbil and Dohuk Governorates.

[40] World Bank, *The Kurdistan Region of Iraq: Assessing the Economic and Social Impact of the Syrian Conflict and ISIS*, World Bank Publications (2015), p. 7-11.

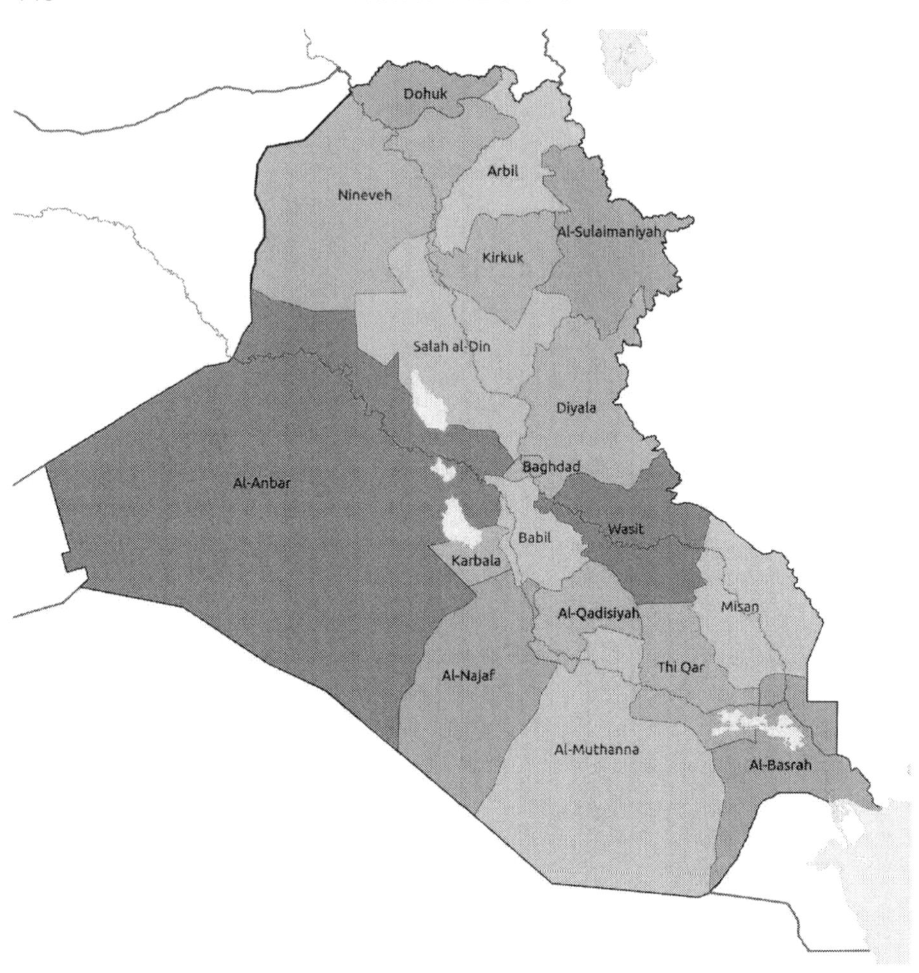

Figure 3. Map of Iraqi Governorates. Source: Wikimedia Commons

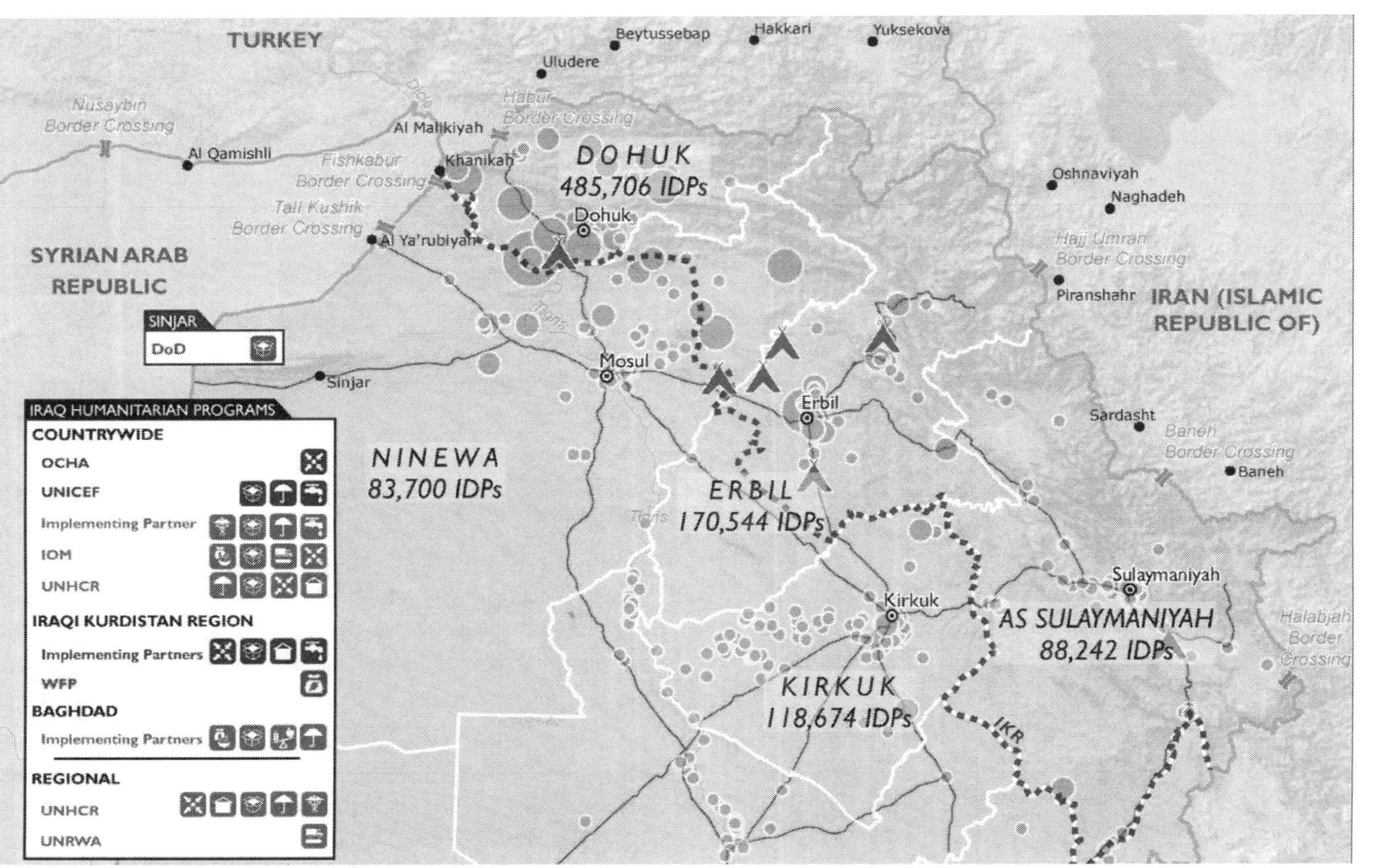
TURKEY
SYRIAN ARAB REPUBLIC
IRAN (ISLAMIC REPUBLIC OF)
DOHUK
485,706 IDPs
ERBIL
170,544 IDPs
KIRKUK
118,674 IDPs
AS SULAYMANIYAH
88,242 IDPs
NINEWA
83,700 IDPs
IKR
Beytussebap
Hakkari
Yuksekova
Uludere
Nusaybin Border Crossing
Habur Border Crossing
Al Malikiyah
Al Qamishli
Fishkabur Border Crossing
Khanikah
Tall Kushik Border Crossing
Al Ya'rubiyah
Dohuk
Mosul
Sinjar
Erbil
Kirkuk
Sulaymaniyah
Oshnaviyah
Naghadeh
Haji Umran Border Crossing
Piranshahr
Sardasht
Baneh Border Crossing
Baneh
Halabjah Border Crossing
SINJAR
DoD
IRAQ HUMANITARIAN PROGRAMS
COUNTRYWIDE
OCHA
UNICEF
Implementing Partner
IOM
UNHCR
IRAQI KURDISTAN REGION
Implementing Partners
WFP
BAGHDAD
Implementing Partners
REGIONAL
UNHCR
UNRWA

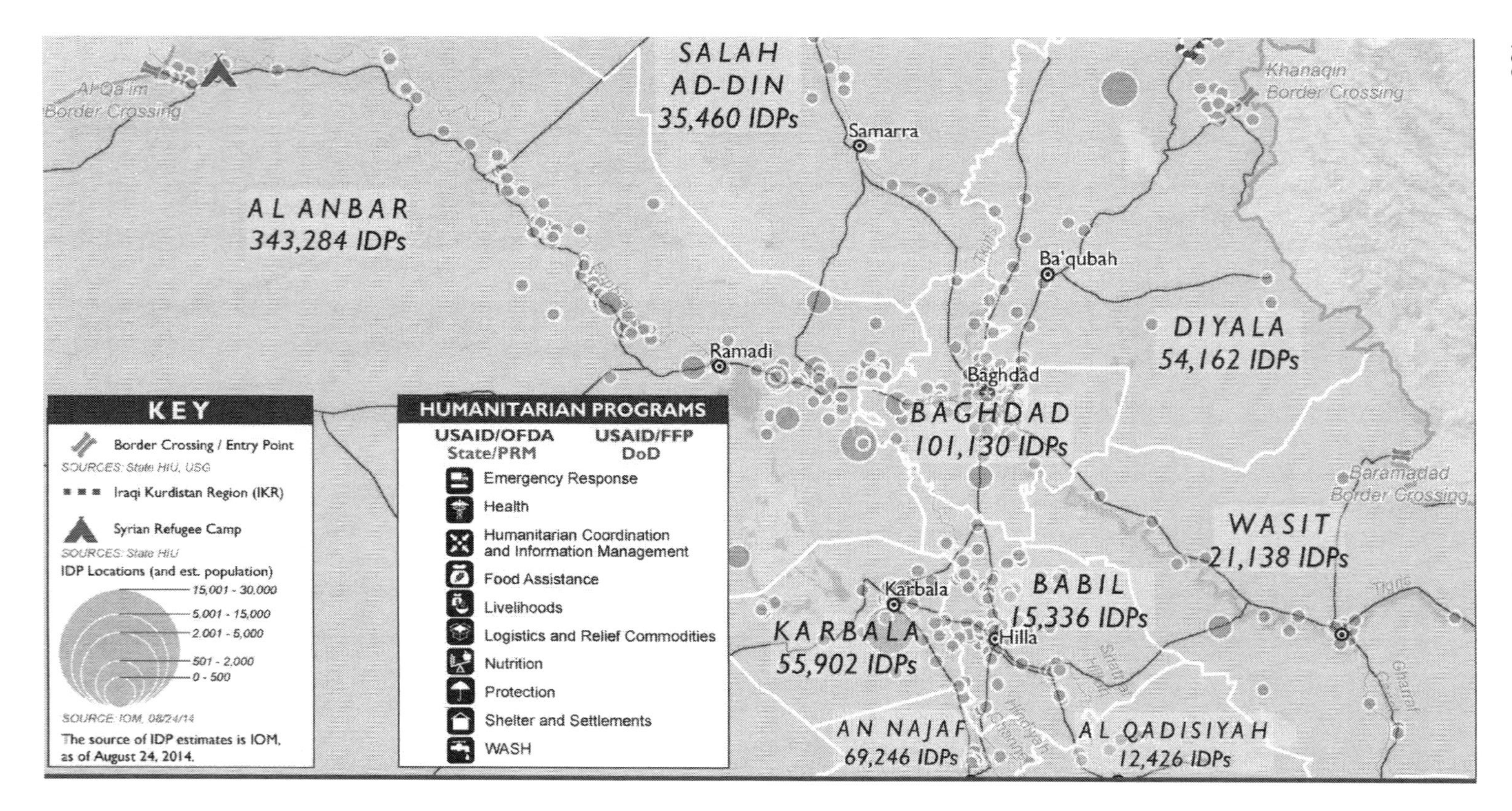

Figure 4. Internally-displaced persons and refugees in Iraq. This map demonstrates the major cities and regions that host internally-displaced Iraqis as well as Syrian refugee camps. Internally-displaced persons are most concentrated throughout Iraq's Kurdistan Region. Source: USAID, USG Humanitarian Assistance - Iraq - Complex Emergency (last updated 28/08/2014)

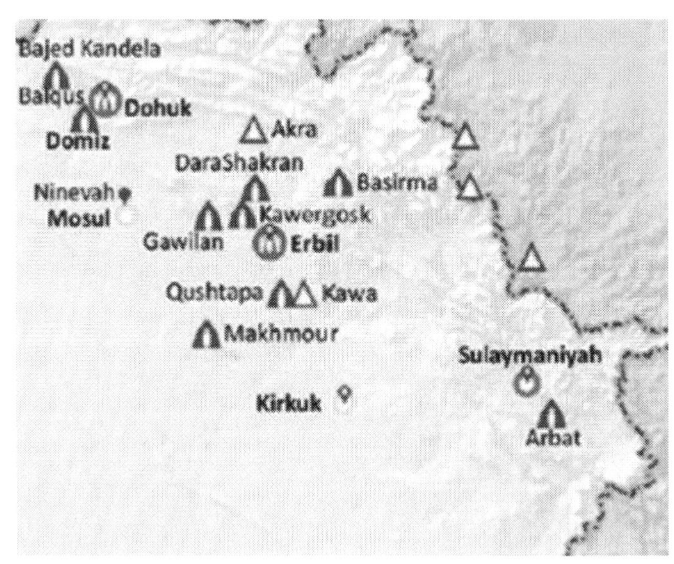

Source: Esri

Figure 5. Map of refugee camps in Erbil and Dohuk Governorates, including the "big four" Erbil camps: Darashakran, Kawergosk, Qushtapa and Basirma. Other notable camps displayed include: Makhmour Camp, also in the Erbil Governorate, near the border of the Kirkuk Governorate; Domiz Camp in the Dohuk Governorate and Arbat Camp in the Sulaymaniyah Governorate.

B. The Refugee Crisis in Erbil

1. Introduction to Erbil

Erbil is a city of contrasts. On the one hand, it is a major business center and commercial hub hosting multinational conglomerates, major energy firms and international law firms, all having established a presence in Erbil following Kurdistan's unparalleled economic growth. Its two commercial airports, Erbil International Airport and Sulaymaniyah International Airport, welcome a heavy flow of not only business executives and contractors, but also tourists drawn to Erbil's rich cultural heritage and centuries-old citadels, castles, monasteries and mosques.

On the other hand, Erbil borders Iraq's Nineveh Governorate, a province that has been largely occupied by IS and one that has witnessed some of the most egregious violations of international law in modern times. Women, children and other civilians who have been raped, tortured, forcibly married and in some cases, enslaved, have fled their homes to find refuge in Erbil, which now hosts over 100,000 refugees and internally-displaced persons.

According to UNHCR, the greatest majority of these persons—81,339 individuals or 35,213 households—are based in Erbil outside of the formal camps. Residence of the remaining individuals is divided between the various refugee camps, with the greatest number residing in Darashakran and Kawergosk Refugee Camps.

Figure 6. The displacement of Kurds in northern Iraq is the most recent trial to be faced by the Kurds, survivors of ethnic cleansing and victims of chemical weapons. This photograph depicts Kurdish refugees traveling by truck between their mountain campsites and tent cities established by the US military in 1991 to aid Kurds who fled the forces of Saddam Hussein in northern Iraq. Credit: US Department of Defense

2. The Camps

a) *Darashakran Refugee Camp*

A one-hour drive northwest of Erbil and fifteen minutes northeast of Kawergosk Camp, hosts 10,381 registered Syrian refugees.[41] The majority of the Camp's refugees are Syrian Kurds from the northeastern city of Qamishli. A significant number of refugees are Syrian Arabs hailing from the northwestern cities of Syria, including Aleppo and its neighboring towns and villages.

---

[41] Syria Regional Refugee Response, Inter-agency Information Sharing Portal, Iraq, Erbil, Darashakran Camp, "Total Persons of Concern," UNHCR – The UN Refugee Agency, available at <http://data.unhcr.org/syrianrefugees/settlement.php?id=246&country=103®ion=65 > (last accessed 5 Nov. 2015).

View of Darashakran Refugee Camp from its outer gate.

Refugees at the Camp expressed gratitude to the Kurdistan Regional Government (**KRG**) for welcoming them to Iraq with open arms. Suleiman Ahmed 'Aza, a Syrian Kurd from the city of Qamishli, said that in Kurdistan, he felt he was living among brothers and sisters. Yet despite the hospitality of his Kurdish hosts, he cited the many hardships of living in a refugee camp, including shortages of food and water and the inadequacy of UNHCR's stipend of IQD 11,000 (USD 9.97) per person per month. He also cited deficiencies in medical care, pointing to the death of his one-month old infant due to a heart deficiency that could have been prevented with proper access to medical care.

Despite these hardships, Suleiman prefers remaining in Iraq over returning to Syria, where aerial bombardments in his neighborhood destroyed his neighbor's apartment, and sent Suleiman and his family fleeing to Iraq nearly two years ago.

Suleiman Ahmed 'Aza poses with his wife and two of his eight children.

Part of the issue being faced by Suleiman and his family is the overcrowding at Darashakran Refugee Camp, a problem shared by other camps in Iraqi Kurdistan. The year 2015 saw an influx of refugees that brought the Camp well over its initial planned capacity for 10,000 refugees.

UNHCR works hand in hand with various UN agencies, such as UNICEF, and international NGOs, including the NRC, in providing education, food and shelter at Darashakran Refugee Camp. Among its other activities, the NRC hosts a community center that provides Camp residents a safe place to interact, play board games, enroll in language classes and professional skills courses and play sports. The center aims to build a sense of community between refugees and humanitarian relief workers through a variety of recreational activities. As a result of this interaction, a sense of trust is built between refugees and aid workers. It is often in this context that victims of gender-based violence (**GBV**) open up to NRC staff, sharing traumas they may have experienced while living in camps. This first point of contact is often the first step to providing the victim with social counseling, support and protection.

Syrian refugee children enjoy a competitive game of soccer at NRC's community center at Darashakran Refugee Camp.

A Syrian refugee beneficiary and NRC aid worker play a board game at NRC's community center.

b) Kawergosk Refugee Camp

(1) Overview

A 40-minute drive northwest of Erbil and fifteen minutes southwest of Darashakran Camp, Kawergosk Refugee Camp hosts 10,094 registered Syrian refugees.[42] Kawergosk Refugee Camp has experienced severe overcrowding as refugees have continued to cross the Syrian border after the Camp's capacity for 2,000 tents had already been filled. With the new arrivals in late 2014, there are about 2,500 tents in the Camp, far over the Camp's planned capacity. Only 60% of the households at Kawergosk Refugee Camp live in adequate dwellings.[43]

Today, many refugees live in the outskirts of the Camp, where they fall outside of formal aid distribution. Scores of refugees complain of hunger, especially since a World Food Programme voucher program was discontinued in early summer of 2015 following budget cuts.

(2) Children

The most significant challenge faced by children at Kawergosk include lack of access to education, with the largest barriers being lack of appropriate school levels for children, especially in the higher secondary grades, and the requirement for older children to work. At the time of this writing, only 56% of children were enrolled in camp schools, with 52% receiving school supplies.[44]

---

[42] Syria Regional Refugee Response, Inter-agency Information Sharing Portal, Iraq, Erbil, Kawergosk Camp, "Total Persons of Concern," UNHCR – The UN Refugee Agency, available at <http://data.unhcr.org/syrianrefugees/settlement.php?id=239®ion=65&country=103> (last accessed 5 Nov. 2015).

[43] "Kawergosk Refugee Camp Profile," UNHCR, the UN Refugee Agency (31 Dec. 2014), available at <http://data.unhcr.org/syrianrefugees/download.php?id=8446> (last accessed 22 Dec. 2015).

[44] *Id.*

Sisters Rayan and Rawan suffer from plugged eye ducts, which will be treated by an operation to be provided by *Médecins Sans Frontières* (Doctors without Borders). Refugee children living outside of the Camp boundaries are not so fortunate to have access to free medical intervention.

(3) Profiles of Refugee Families

Hassan Muslim Mustafa fled from his home in Kobani (Ayn al-Arab), in the Aleppo Governorate of Syria, in the fall of 2014, after Kawergosk's capacity to host refugees had already been filled. Since then, he has been living outside of the Camp's borders, where he and his family have been the last to receive aid.

Hassan Muslim Mustafa poses with his family just outside of Kawergosk Refugee Camp's formal border. Like many of his Syrian neighbors, Hassan's chief complaint was, "I am hungry; I have no work; I have no food."

Since World Food Programme vouchers were discontinued in the summer of 2015, Hassan has been reduced to begging for food. As of December of 2015, he had accrued USD 1,300 of debt just to purchase food, water and other basic provisions to ensure the survival of his family.

Having arrived to Kawergosk Refugee Camp in November of 2014, Abu Ahmed lives in one of the 500 tents not serviced by UN agencies and international NGOs. Outside of the formal Camp boundaries, elderly refugees such as Abu Ahmed have no access to medical attention, unless they have adequate resources to pay for private medical care.

c) *Other Camps*

Other smaller refugee camps in the Erbil Governorate include Qushtapa Refugee Camp, which is approximately two-and-a-half hours by car south of Erbil, with 6,666 registered Syrian refugees,[45] and Basirma Refugee Camp, which is approximately three hours northeast of Erbil by car, with 3,465 registered Syrian refugees.[46]

---

[45] Syria Regional Refugee Response, Inter-agency Information Sharing Portal, Iraq, Erbil, Qushtapa Camp, "Total Persons of Concern," UNHCR – The UN Refugee Agency, available at <http://data.unhcr.org/syrianrefugees/settlement.php?id=244&country=103®ion=65 > (last accessed on 7 Nov. 2015).

[46] Syria Regional Refugee Response, Inter-agency Information Sharing Portal, Iraq, Erbil, Basirma Camp, "Total Persons of Concern," UNHCR – The UN Refugee Agency, available at <http://data.unhcr.org/syrianrefugees/settlement.php?id=242&country=103®ion=65 > (last accessed on 7 Nov. 2015).

C. The Refugee Crisis Dohuk

1. Domiz Refugee Camp: An Overview

Located in the Dohuk region, approximately 150 kilometers (93 miles) northwest of Erbil, Domiz Refugee Camp is divided into two districts: Domiz 1 Camp, which hosts over 40,000 Syrian refugees,[47] and Domiz 2 Camp, which hosts over 6,000.[48] These numbers starkly contrast anticipated needs when the Camp was first designed to host about 2,000 families. Part of this overcrowding is due to the Camp's proximity to the Syrian border, thus making it one of the first camps available to refugees fleeing Syria.

As a result of overcrowding, Domiz Refugee Camp cannot accept new arrivals. Consequently, newly-arriving refugees have begun erecting temporary shelters outside of the formal Camp boundaries. Many of these refugees remain on waiting lists to be relocated to the formal campgrounds.

---

[47] Syria Regional Refugee Response, Inter-agency Information Sharing Portal, Iraq, Duhok, Domiz 1 Camp, "Total Persons of Concern," UNHCR – The UN Refugee Agency, available at <http://data.unhcr.org/syrianrefugees/settlement.php?id=254&country=103®ion=63> (last accessed on 5 Nov. 2015).

[48] Syria Regional Refugee Response, Inter-agency Information Sharing Portal, Iraq, Duhok, Domiz 2 Camp, "Total Persons of Concern," UNHCR – The UN Refugee Agency, available at <http://data.unhcr.org/syrianrefugees/settlement.php?id=266&country=103®ion=63> (last accessed on 5 Nov. 2015).

Water and sanitation facilities at Domiz Refugee Camp remain insufficient to meet the demand of the number of Syrian refugees that have been received. Photograph: NRC/Christian Jepsen

2. Standards and Indicators

UNHCR reports an adequate quality and quantity of food assistance provided through food vouchers redeemable in retail shops in Domiz. Refugees also have access to a primary health center, two satellite health posts and a maternity ward.[49]

However, there are many challenges to life at Domiz Refugee Camp. The Camp now suffers from water scarcity and, due to the influx of internally-displaced persons, only the needs of the most vulnerable populations are met. Not all refugees receive Core Relief Item kits, including winterization items, though all refugees receive kerosene for heating.[50]

One of the major challenges faced in the Domiz Refugee Camp is education, with the major impediment being the lack of appropriate school levels for children. This issue Is especially concentrated in the higher secondary schools. A second issue that stands in the way of education is the need for many older children to work to support their families.[51]

[49] "Domiz 1 Refugee Camp Profile," UNHCR (31 Dec. 2014), available for download from < http://data.unhcr.org/syrianrefugees/settlement.php?id=254&country=103®ion=63> (last accessed 10 Nov. 2015).

[50] *Id.*

[51] *Id.*

The lack of appropriate school levels for children is one of the impediments to adequate educational services at Domiz Refugee Camp. Photograph: NRC/Christian Jepsen

According to UNHCR, Domiz Refugee Camp adequately meets WASH standards and indicators, with households having private latrines and showers. Photograph: NRC/Christian Jepsen

D. Internally-Displaced Persons of Nineveh

While the Syrian refugee crisis dominates headlines, little attention is given to Iraq's own IDP population. Yet it is impossible to discuss the Syrian refugee crisis in Iraq without also treating Iraq's IDP crisis. To give perspective to the gravity of the IDP crisis, while there are currently approximately 250,000 Syrian refugees living in Iraq,[52] there are more than 15 times as many—at least 4 million—internally-displaced Iraqis.[53]

These IDPs are inextricably linked to the Syrian refugee crisis. Both Syrian refugees and Iraqi IDPs are the indirect result of a Syrian civil war that has created a power vacuum in certain pockets of Eastern Syria, which has led to the rise of militant groups such as ISIS that have in turn caused the displacement of millions of Syrians and Iraqis. In this chapter, we will examine these IDPs, with a focus on two of the religious minorities that have been specifically targeted by ISIS: Yazidis and Christians.

1. Yazidis

ISIS's conquest of territory throughout Nineveh Governorate has displaced thousands of Yazidis. These Yazidi IDPs, who now live in Dohuk and Erbil, are discussed below.

a) Yazidi Families in Erbil: Madrasat Ashtar Camp

Erbil's landscape is riddled with informal Yazidi settlements, normally comprised of improvised tents set up in parking lots, parks and other open areas. Madrasat Ashtar Camp, located just behind Madrasat Ashtar (Ashtar school), hosts 48 Yazidi families (over 200 individuals) that are supported by Caritas Internationalis, Samaritan's Purse and a local church, which distribute food and support the Yazidis financially.

Yazidi families spoke of ISIS's brutality in having slaughtered hundreds of Yazidi men upon arriving to Yazidi towns and villages and then forcing their wives and daughters into marriage and, in some cases, slavery. The refugees at Madrasat Ashtar Camp managed to flee villages near Mosul prior to ISIS's occupation.

---

[52] "Numbers and locations of Syrian refugees and IDPs," US Department of State. Sources - US Department of State (Humanitarian Information Unit), USAID, UN OCHA, UNHCR, UNRWA (17 Apr. 2015).

[53] "Iraq IDP Figures Analysis," IDMC, Internal Displacement Monitoring Center (15 June 2015), available at <http://www.internal-displacement.org/middle-east-and-north-africa/iraq/figures-analysis>.

b) *Yazidi Women: SEED Foundation*

Yazidi women have been subject to some of the most heinous crimes that have transpired since the onset of the Syrian civil war. In response, SEED Foundation (**SEED**), a registered charity based in Akre in the Dohuk Governorate, has established a Women's Cooperative Center to treat, support and address the needs of displaced Yazidi women.

(1) Overview of SEED

SEED is one of many civil society initiatives working towards development in Kurdistan. The organization is based in Mamilyan Camp, a camp comprised of approximately 13,000 IDPs, approximately 80% of which are Yazidis who fled Sinjar and Mosul to escape the brutal takeover of those areas by ISIS. The remaining 20% are Shabak, Harki and Zebari Muslims.

SEED's mission is to promote Kurdistan's social, educational and economic development to address the humanitarian needs and protect the human rights of the residents of Kurdistan. To this end, SEED partners with and financially supports other organizations active in delivering assistance in Kurdistan and provides humanitarian assistance to Kurdistan's refugee population to promote their welfare, safety and education.

Given the almost unimaginable abuses perpetrated against the Yazidi community, rates of trauma at Mamilyan Camp are high and there is a critical need for psychological services to help survivors begin to heal. SEED provides these much-needed psychotherapy and social-work services, as well as training, education and recreation opportunities to those in need, with a focus on Yazidi women and girls who are survivors of sexual violence. SEED's Women's Cooperative Center provides livelihood training, psycho-social services, medical clinics and classes and promotes activities to strengthen the family unit and rebuild family relationships.

(2) Profile of an ISIS survivor

Faiza was 17-years-old when ISIS stormed her village, separated the men and the women and took her and other girls and women from the village by force. She can still hear the gunmen saying, "Take the women and kill the men!" She replays these words in her mind. She saw an ISIS fighter holding a gun to her husband's head. She begged and pleaded with the gunman to spare her husband's life. Her husband managed to escape.

"We knew what was going to happen when we were under the hands of ISIS. So I would rather have killed myself before they killed me...," she said. Later Faiza and her sister-in-law managed to escape from ISIS.

While in captivity, she saw with her own eyes people beheaded and burned. She prays to God that she can forget the things she saw, but says that it is "impossible for these memories to go away." Her mother-in-law said Faiza gets angry all the time, throws things and has tried to hurt herself. Like many who were abducted before her, she struggles to escape terrifying memories and the psychological toll they have had on her.

While in captivity, Faiza, an ISIS survivor, witnessed beheadings and immolations.

2. Christians

a) Overview

ISIS's conquest of Mosul and its neighboring cities, towns and villages, including Qaraqosh, sent thousands of Christians fleeing to the Erbil Governorate. Most of these refugees fled just prior to ISIS's arrival. Having heard of the atrocities committed by ISIS against Iraqi Yazidis, many Christians escaped before ISIS had an opportunity to seize their women, forcibly marry their daughters and enslave their children.

Today, Christian IDPs reside in camps as well as in urban centers throughout Erbil. Those in urban centers often reside in homes and apartments paid for by local churches with the support of foreign churches and individual donors.

Youth at Ankawa Assembly Church in Erbil put on a play for their local community depicting their escape from Mosul. Entitled "What Was Our Offence?," the play expresses the feelings of many youth who now find themselves displaced and uprooted from their communities for no fault of their own.

b) Ankawa 2 Camp

Ankawa 2 Camp, also referred to as Ashti Camp, is managed by Fr. Ammanoel Adel Kalo and run by the Assyrian Catholic Church.[54] A host of international NGOs, including SOS Chrétiens d'Orient, Caritas Internationalis, Samaritan's Purse, Mennonite Central Committee, SALT Foundation Holland, MISEREOR Ihr Hilfswerk and Movimento Shalom onlus, operate at the Camp, providing aid, supplies and provisions to IDPs.

As of December 2015, the Camp hosts 5,500 Christian IDPs living in 1,000 caravans. The Camp continues to receive entry petitions from new IDPs every month, but the Camp has already reached its full capacity. Fr. Ammanoel considers the only durable solution to the conflict to be resettlement to third countries. He has had some success in linking up refugee families with host countries. As of December 2015, the Czech Republic, for example, had agreed to accept 18 Ankawa 2 Camp refugees to be resettled by the end of 2015. However, such numbers represent a small percentage of the Iraqi IDPs seeking to resettle. Fr. Ammanoel believes that resettlement offers from stable nations are the best type of aid that can be provided to IDPs.[55]

Like most caravans at Ankawa 2 Camp, this caravan bears the sign of the cross.

[54] For Fact Sheet, see <https://www.humanitarianresponse.info/en/system/files/documents/files/reach_irq_factsheet_ankawa_2_idp_camp_profile_september2015_0.pdf>.

[55] Interview with Fr. Ammanoel Adel Kalo, Ankawa 2 Camp, Erbil (16 Dec. 2015).

The conditions and quality of life at Ankawa 2 Camp surpass those of the Syrian refugee camps. Refugees live in caravans rather than tents; roads are paved rather than covered with slippery mud; educational enrollment among six- to eleven-year olds is near 90% rather than 50%; 95% of families receive family food parcels or their equivalent; and 100% of households accessed shelter assistance since arrival at the Camp.[56]

Despite these metrics, IDPs complain about their prospects for the future. Living in a two-room caravan is no substitute for the large villas that many IDPs previously occupied. They were able to come and go as they pleased, start businesses and build their futures and those of their children. With no end to the Iraqi IDP crisis in sight, some residents lamented of the uncertainty they face. These IDPs conceded that their plight was better than that of the Syrian refugees, but still, they said, living in a caravan indefinitely was no way to build one's life or future.

Sayed Sabah, the headmaster of the Ankawa 2 Camp elementary school and a member of the Camp's central committeee, speaks of abandoning homes and property in Qaraqosh, all of which are currently occupied by ISIS, before reaching Ankawa 2 Camp in April 2015.

[56] "Ankawa 2 Camp Profile," Erbil Governorate, Iraq, REACH Initiative (Sept. 2015), available at <https://www.humanitarianresponse.info/en/system/files/documents/files/reach_irq_factsheet_ankawa_2_idp_camp_profile_september2015_0.pdf> (last accessed 22 Dec. 2015).

Umm Michel attempts to make the best life she can living in a crammed caravan. She poses next to a sewing machine that she uses to scrap together a living at Ankawa 2 Camp.

E. Challenges to Durable Solutions

1. Financial Challenges

In a meeting organized by the USKBC, Foreign Minister Falah M. Bakir explained the context of Iraqi Kurdistan's warm reception of Syrian refugees. He expressed empathy with the plight of Syrian refugees, stating that the Kurds "feel the Syrians' pain" because the Kurds themselves have been refugees and IDPs. However, he lamented a humanitarian crisis that limited KRG resources are ill-equipped to address. He longed for a durable solution to the Syrian civil war that would plug the refugee influx.[57]

Minister of the Interior Karim Sinjari affirmed that the Kurdish government would not close off the border through which Syrian refugees have been pouring into Iraq. However, he emphasized that Iraqi Kurdistan was taking on the lion's share of what should be a "shared responsibility." He cited Iraqi Kurdistan's own IDP crisis and the challenge of battling ISIS. The KRG is feeling the impact of a war whose front line stretches 1,050 kilometers. Currently, 7,800 wounded Peshmerga fighters require medical attention. Waging the war with ISIS is depleting financial resources, especially with the central government in Baghdad and the international community so reluctant to directly arm and fund Iraqi Kurdistan's military forces. The financial crisis has been so acute that in some months, the KRG has been unable to pay all government employee salaries.[58]

2. Challenges in the Battle against ISIS

In defending the front line against ISIS, the Peshmerga faces a host of challenges, the most critical of which is inadequate funding, insufficient armaments and obsolete weaponry. While ISIS wields advanced automatic weapons, many Peshmerga fighters are carrying decades-old Soviet Kalashnikovs developed in the Cold War era.

---

[57] Meeting with KRG Foreign Minister Falah M. Bakar, the Department of Foreign Relations, Erbil, Iraq, 16 Dec. 2015.

[58] Meeting with KRG Minister of Interior Karim Sinjari, Ministry of the Interior, Erbil, Iraq, 17 Dec. 2015.

Many Peshmerga fighters are ill-equipped in the battle against ISIS. Inadequate and obsolete weaponry impede their ability to definitively defeat ISIS. Photograph: Kenneth D'Alessandro

Political divisions within Iraq and tensions between Iraq's central government and the KRG has resulted in Baghdad's failure to properly arm and fund the Peshmerga. Part of this is due to the Kurds' longstanding ambition for autonomy and, as some would say, statehood, which many in Baghdad see as inconsistent with the interests of greater Iraq. The central government of Iraq is thus as cautious with the Kurds as are the governments of Turkey and Iran, where a significant number of Kurds also reside.

The United States, for its part, currently maintains a "one-Iraq policy," which means that all military assistance is channeled through Baghdad. To the detriment of the Kurds, this often results in the failure of military assistance to reach Iraqi Kurdistan, where it is desperately needed.

Minister of the Interior Karim Sinjari has stressed Kurdistan's need for heavy weaponry, tanks, armored vehicles and air support in confronting ISIS, whose arsenal includes some of the world's most advanced weaponry, including US-made Humvees plundered from the Iraqi army.[59] Similarly needed on the front line are bomb detectors and robots to remove and detonate mines left by ISIS in villages recaptured by the Peshmerga. Until the Peshmerga receives such technology and is trained to operate them, its ability to recapture ISIS-held territory will be extremely limited.

Kurdish ceremony on the front line celebrating Flag Day on 17 December 2015.

[59] *Id.*

Part III. Corporate Partnerships and Civil Society Initiatives

Chapter 6. Introduction

A. A Global Crisis

It would be easy to dismiss the Syrian refugee crisis as just another Middle Eastern problem, one that should be addressed by the Arab League or the Syrian people themselves. Why should we be concerned, many ask, with a matter rooted halfway across the world? Why should we care? We should care because the refugee crisis is not just an internal Syrian issue, nor even a merely Middle Eastern problem. Rather, the Syrian refugee crisis is a *global* problem in every sense of the word.

When we are accosted by images of starving civilians trapped in besieged cities, we all have a duty to act, no matter how distant or remote the suffering may be from us. When innocent men, women, girls and boys are washed up on beaches like discarded rubbish in their attempt to desperately escape mass atrocities, their problems become our own. When a nation is engulfed in armed conflict so vicious that images of still, lifeless children become the staple of media covering the conflict, we all have a responsibility to act.

B. Am I My Brother's Keeper?

In responding to the bloodshed today being witnessed in Syria, we are confronted with a question: Am I my brother's keeper? In responding to images of human suffering, our first choice is to turn a blind eye. After all, we have our own problems to deal with. Our second choice is to respond to the images as though their subjects were our own mothers and fathers, brothers and sisters, sons and daughters, husbands and wives—when a Syrian child is robbed of his family and is left fending for himself in the streets of Istanbul or Beirut, it is as though our own child has been robbed, left to fend for himself in a cold, indifferent world; when a Syrian refugee has been displaced and rendered homeless three times, each time by a new crisis or armed group, it is as though our own brother has been rendered homeless; when a Syrian mother is on the verge of death, about to leave her children as orphans, because she cannot afford medicine for an otherwise curable disease, it is as though our own mother is on the verge of death. It means viewing all of humanity as the victims of the Syrian crisis; if one Syrian suffers, we all suffer with him.

The response to the question, "Am I my brother's keeper?" is an unequivocal "yes." This answer is not based merely on abstract moral or ethical principles; our responsibility to protect is firmly founded on legal principles as well. The international community has come together and ratified countless treaties undertaking to not only refrain from violating basic human rights, but also to ensure the protection of such rights. Consider, for example, the International Covenant on Civil and Political Rights (**ICCPR**), which requires States party to not only refrain from violating basic rights such as the right to life (Art. 6 ICCPR), freedom of thought, conscience and religion (Art. 18 ICCPR), but also to ensure the protection of these rights from other member States' violations (Art. 2(3) ICCPR), thus incorporating an affirmative duty to act. Similarly, the Convention on the Prevention and Punishment of the Crime of Genocide (**CPPG**) requires not only that its 140 States party refrain from carrying out the crime of genocide, but also that they "undertake to prevent and to punish" genocide (Art. I CPPG). How, then, can anyone respond to the attempted extermination of religious minorities, including Christians and Yazidis in occupied Syria and Iraq, retorting with indifference, "Am I my brother's keeper?"

In reaffirming our common humanity, we must view every Syrian—whether Alawi, Christian, Druze, Shi'ite or Sunni; whether Arab, Assyrian, Circassian, Kurdish or Turkic—as our neighbor, and commit to treat that neighbor as ourselves. When confronted with images that shock our conscience, we must invest our time, talents and resources in freeing Syria from the scourge that ravages her people.

What can we do? How can we help Syria? How can we alleviate the suffering of nearly 12 million displaced persons? As we will see, the possibilities for engagement are limited only by the imagination. The purpose of the next three chapters is to explore how ordinary individuals who may not have any specialized training or experience in humanitarian relief may contribute to the assistance and protection of the Syrian people. As we will see, there is a role for each of us to play. This role can be as simple as writing a check, but it can be much more than this. Whether you are an architect, attorney, business owner, carpenter, doctor, engineer, entrepreneur, IT technician, journalist, paramedic, photographer, teacher or web developer, there is a role you can play in relieving suffering and restoring normalcy to lives impacted by war.

Chapter 7. Partnerships with Humanitarian Agencies

In this section, we explore partnerships that flourished and serve as examples for future replication as well as partnerships that failed at some stage in the conception or execution. From these case studies, we will draw lessons for best practices.

A. Case Studies

1. Public-Private Partnerships at Za'tari Refugee Camp

Professionals in humanitarian assistance have historically drawn a strict dichotomy between the humanitarian and the private sectors. Some professionals in the humanitarian field so dogmatically adhere to this dichotomy that they refuse corporate partnerships altogether. Today, however, given the gravity of humanitarian crises around the globe and the growing recognition of the inability of governments, international organizations and humanitarian NGOs to tackle these crises on their own, the private sector is emerging as a necessary partner in humanitarian assistance and protection.

Increasingly, international NGOs rely on the private sector for both funding and contributions of know-how and expertise. A Norwegian Refugee Council Shelter Project Coordinator at Za'tari Refugee Camp has commented on the changing landscape of international humanitarian assistance, as companies and other private sector actors more actively partner with governments and NGOs.[60]

For Kilian Kleinschmit, the former UNHCR Head of the Mafraq Sub-Office and Za'atari Camp Manager, these contributions of expertise are at least as important as funding. Kilian has thus been active and successful at securing key partnerships with the private sector, governments and other actors. Examples of partnerships at Za'tari Refugee Camp vary widely. The City of Amsterdam has recently partnered with the Camp to provide energy, transportation and master planning, investing USD 1.4 million. SunEdison is partnering with the Camp to design a renewable energy / solar farm project, which will help the Camp offset USD 700,000 in monthly electricity expenses.

---

[60] Personal interview conducted on 7 Apr., 2014. The Shelter Project Coordinator requested that his name be anonymized due to ongoing sensitivities and security issues.

Megan Smith, vice president of Google[x] at Google, visited the camp to discuss new partnerships to bring Internet connectivity to refugees.

Kilian Kleinschmit, the Za'atari Camp Manager, discusses the importance of public-private partnerships to secure contributions of expertise in the fields of planning and infrastructure.

Other partnerships include those aimed at social development, sports and community. For example, FC Bayern Munich, among the largest soccer clubs in the world, organized a football camp to train Syrian girls. A UK team visited the Camp to provide training to community police.

Yet these partnerships represent just a fraction of the number of offers that UNHCR receives on a monthly basis from the private sector and civil society. Kilian has cited countless offers from companies, churches, NGOs and other civil society actors and an inability to keep up with the demand. In fact, private sector offers of assistance often fail to come to fruition with UNHCR; like many other UN agencies and international NGOs, it does not have the machinery to take in private offers of assistance and channel them into concrete projects.

For this reason, UNHCR will be launching an "Innovation and Planning Unit" that will have three to four dedicated staff members on site at Za'tari Refugee Camp that will serve as an intake unit to match assistance offers with present needs. Kilian hopes the Unit will foster a global network of partners that will improve the lives of refugees and restore their dignity.

Elrashid H. Hammad, the World Food Programme's (WFP) Head of the Mafraq Sub-Office, points to a poster that lists WFP partner organizations and governments, including the European Union, the United Nations and the governments of the United States, Switzerland, Sweden, Japan and Canada.

2. The Dentons-Norwegian Refugee Council Partnership

In my April 2014 visit to Za'tari Refugee Camp, I discovered the tremendous need among humanitarian agency programs for private sector knowledge and expertise. A prime example is the NRC's Information, Counseling and Legal Assistance (**ICLA**) program, which provides legal counsel on the local laws of the countries in which refugees are residing, including Jordan, Lebanon and Iraq. Even if the NRC had on its staff the most preeminent of international lawyers, such lawyers would be unable to guide the NRC on Jordanian, Lebanese or Iraqi law unless the lawyers actually lived in the respective jurisdictions, worked with local authorities and fully understood the content and the application of such laws. If the NRC were to recruit the most accomplished of international lawyers, the organization would perhaps be able to rely on them to comment, for example, on the requirement under the Geneva Conventions to allow the free passage of humanitarian aid consignments in times of armed conflict or the application of objective or subjective criteria to the principle of *non-refoulement* under the Refugee Convention. But could such an expert comment on the legal and administrative framework governing the deportation of asylum seekers from

Jordan? What about the due process rights of foreign nationals to challenge Iraqi deportation decisions? Could they comment, for example, on the requirements for obtaining a building permit in Lebanon and whether these requirements change if the applicant is a Syrian or Palestinian refugee, or on the procedural formalities for establishing a legal NGO presence in Turkey? By and large, the answer is a firm "no."

An organization in the NRC's position has several options. It may seek the services of an international law firm experienced in the laws of Jordan, Lebanon, Turkey and beyond, thereby incurring legal fees ranging from USD 300 to 800 per hour, thus diverting funds that could otherwise be dedicated to programs. Alternatively, the NRC can hire legal officers licensed in the countries in which it is operating, further committing funds to their salaries and upkeep. Third, the NRC can engage a law firm with a commitment to corporate social responsibility (**CSR**) to issue advice on a pro bono basis.

The NRC has adopted a hybrid approach whereby it both hires legal specialists to manage its ICLA programs across the Middle East and has simultaneously engaged Dentons to provide legal counsel on a pro bono basis. In 2014, Dentons signed a letter of engagement with the NRC to provide pro bono advice on local laws governing landlord-tenant relations, birth and marriage registrations, deportation and other administrative decisions, foreigner registration and housing, land and property rights as they impact Syrian refugees residing in the Middle East. Following a successful pilot in Jordan, the program was expanded in 2015 to Lebanon, then Iraq and, finally, Turkey.

Today, Dentons' partnership with the NRC is continually expanding beyond the provision of pro bono legal services in Jordan, Lebanon, Iraq and Turkey. Dentons is currently facilitating high level meetings between the NRC and one of Qatar's most prominent foundations through the contact of a firm client. Dentons is further exploring potential avenues to fundraise for the NRC in a way that complies with NGO-related legislation in Qatar and the United Arab Emirates, as well as sending volunteers to work with refugees on the ground throughout the region, thereby exemplifying corporate citizenship by giving back to the communities in the international markets in which it operates.

B. Lessons Learned

As the partnerships at Za'tari Refugee Camp and the Dentons-NRC partnership clearly demonstrate, in-kind donations are often as valuable as cash contributions. This is particularly the case when knowledge and expertise is leveraged to establish an infrastructure that multiplies the impact on refugee advancement and protection—for example, a sanitation platform that pays dividends into the future by reducing disease or an Internet connectivity project that gives refugees opportunities to earn income through e-commerce.

The Dentons-NRC partnership is successful because it leverages the specific strengths of Dentons with the needs of the NRC. The partnership would not boast this success if Dentons did not have a presence in Lebanon,

Jordan and the other jurisdictions in which the NRC operates. In fact, the NRC piloted partnerships with firms having no Middle East presence in the past, and the partnerships resulted in failure. Partnerships thus only flourish when they tap into specific capabilities and match them with present needs.

The possibilities for other companies to leverage their unique capabilities to mimic the Dentons-NRC partnership are limitless. Whether a potential advocacy partner works at a global technology firm as a computer programmer, as a graphic designer at a web design company or as a clean energy specialist at a power corporation, there are unlimited potential partnerships that can be established between companies and humanitarian agencies working with refugees. The key is to identify the specific capabilities that a company can provide and then meet the need of a humanitarian agency acting on the ground with refugees.

C. Challenges Faced

It would be misleading to discuss the success of the Dentons-NRC partnership without highlighting the challenges faced in the partnership's conception. Prior the formation of the Dentons-NRC partnership, a host of assistance offers on the part of Dentons were rebuffed by humanitarian agencies.

1. Challenges in Partnering with the UN: An Anecdote

After my first visit to Za'tari Refugee Camp in 2014, I followed up with a dozen UN agencies and humanitarian NGOs to find out how Dentons could contribute to the assistance of Syrian refugees. I was astonished to find my offers of pro bono assistance met with silence at best and outright rejection at worst. In most cases, my offers were met with bewilderment as to what role a corporate law firm could possibly play in assisting refugees.

One UN officer I approached informed me that the due diligence process for vetting a potential pro bono partner was so cumbersome that he was not even willing to initiate it. As he explained, the process required verifying that none of the clients of the potential partner law firm in any way contravene any UN principles. Thus, if just one client of the law firm were a tobacco company, the UN agency would be unable to enter into a partnership because the representation of tobacco companies is deemed to be inherently incompatible with UN positions on health and safety, as seen by the WHO's Tobacco Free Initiative, for example. The same was true of clients of law firm partners involved in the defense field, including manufacturers of weapons and other armaments.

I challenged the rationale behind this policy decision. Dentons is a law firm with a commitment to the highest standards of ethics and business conduct. Moreover, we are committed to making a positive impact in the communities in which we live and work. Why should our CSR reputation be recriminated by the mere fact that we may count among our thousands of clients a tobacco company or a defense contractor? Are there any large international law firms that could potentially partner with the UN that could state that that they have no such companies as their clients? I doubt that the most ethics- and compliance-driven law firms the world over can honestly answer "yes." This is especially the case of the international law firms with a presence in Dubai or other Arabian Gulf jurisdictions, where so much work is defense-sector driven.

I found in the UN agency's policy an impediment to a potential partnership that would, if approved, reap immeasurable dividends to refugee beneficiaries. At the same time, I found the policy to be in itself incompatible with UN principles. The UN agency with which I had been dialoguing was a program that fell under the General Assembly, which was in turn an organ established by the Charter of the UN. That same Charter permits the use of force as a Chapter VII collective security measure (Art. 42) and for individual and collective self-defense (Art. 51). The same international community that came together to create the UN also recognized that in many cases, measures not involving the use of armed force such as diplomacy and sanctions are ineffective in securing peace. In such cases, the Security Council may take military action as may be necessary to maintain or restore international security (Art. 42). Even peacekeepers are armed with rifles and other theatre weapons in order to deter breaches of the peace. How, then, can a UN agency blacklist the very defense contractors that the UN and governments must rely on when the need to secure peace through the use of force arises?

The officer expressed empathy with my views, but did not want any further debate. He politely closed off the discussion with a firm "no" to the potential partnership with Dentons. The agency's compliance and due diligence procedures, he said, were beyond the scope of his authority.

I walked away from that experience disenchanted. The UN had always been an organization that was to me the epitome of the highest aspirations of humanity, including the advancement of all peoples, the propagation of justice and the protection of fundamental human rights. But here, an officer's interpretation of a policy that supposedly upheld the organization's commitment to non-violent means of conflict resolution prevented aid from reaching beneficiaries.

The UN was the successor of the League of Nations, which was in turn the brainchild of President Woodrow Wilson, an idealist whose commitment to collective security, fair labor conditions, global health and human rights perfectly synchronized with my own vision for world peace. As a UN supporter, I have repeatedly defended the organization against indictments for waste, bureaucracy and ineffectiveness. Nowhere has this been the case more than in the years in which I lived in the United States, where the UN's reputation has been especially tarnished by boundless accusations emanating from conservative think tanks and media outlets.

After my experience in trying to forge a partnership with Dentons, however, I had to seriously reconsider the validity of the charges that critics have levied against the UN. Following the failed conception of a partnership with Dentons, I was left wondering how many other potential partnerships were frustrated because of an inflexible interpretation and application of an ill-conceived policy, leaving potential beneficiaries without assistance.[61]

2. Challenges in Partnership with Private Organizations: An Anecdote

In October 2015, I organized a briefing on the Syrian refugee crisis at a luncheon in Dubai hosted by my law firm. Following that briefing, one of the lawyers that attended expressed an interest in going on a four- to six-week sabbatical, volunteering on a humanitarian mission. He asked for my help in brainstorming as to potential locations for such a sabbatical. I was so pleased by the fruit of this luncheon that I eagerly got to work, contacting every humanitarian agency I knew of working with Syrian refugees.

I re-experienced the astonishment that I first experienced in April 2014 in attempting to set up a partnership at Za'tari Refugee Camp. Once again, my offers of pro bono support were met with silence and indifference. Had I been a recruiter at a global talent agency offering the services of this attorney—one who was perfectly fluent in Arabic and English, had decades of international legal experience, including managerial experience, in multiple jurisdictions, and who had studied in both the Middle East and the West, law firms would have aggressively thrown six- and seven-digit salary offers at me. Yet here I was, offering the services of this pre-eminent lawyer, one of the top-ranked in the GCC region, for pro bono legal services over a four- to six-week sabbatical at no cost to potential recipient organizations. Despite the attractiveness of this offer, I was unable to get a single NGO or international organization to express an interest. Even a US-based organization that specifically advertises community volunteer opportunities to assist refugees in resettlement did not return phone calls or emails. I contacted chapters of this organization as geographically diverse as New York, Salt Lake City, Utah, and Wichita, Kansas, all to no avail. I inquired with volunteer operations officers responsible for cooperation with law firms and for immigration lists of pro bono services, community interpreter trainers, resettlement supervisors and immigration program managers. My emails went unanswered; my phone calls were not returned. The only fruit that came out of all of my research and inquiry was an email to schedule a time to speak with a program officer. After

[61] It is not my intent to judge the entire United Nations system on the basis of a few personal experiences. I of course recognize that the UN offers invaluable services to millions of Syrians whose survival is dependent on aid that can only be provided by a platform as broad as that offered by UN humanitarian agencies, such as UNHCR and UNICEF. Moreover, the UN humanitarian agencies' uncompromising commitment to the principles of humanity, independence, neutrality and impartiality is laudable.
At the same time, however, there are serious flaws in the current humanitarian aid framework that cannot be ignored. In my concern for millions of Syrians whose very lives hang in the balance, I am compelled to relay to readers my personal experiences openly and candidly. If anything, I hope my candor will trigger much-needed debate about how our current humanitarian aid framework can be improved by more freely channeling private sector initiatives and resources to those in need.

making myself available at the proposed time, the program officer failed to join the call.

I was dismayed by the fact that one of the primary organizations responsible for the resettlement of refugees in the United States and their integration into American culture displayed indifference at the offer of pro bono services of a lawyer and managing partner who not only spoke Arabic fluently, but also, being an Arab national, had intimate knowledge of Arab culture. Here was an individual who was able to make an important positive contribution to the integration of Syrian (and other Arab) refugees and asylum seekers into American culture, yet all of my offers were met with silence and indifference.

3. The Norwegian Refugee Council's Initial Skepticism

Even the NRC was initially skeptical of entering into a partnership. NRC's Gulf Office Director expressed reservations on the basis of other law firms with which the NRC had partnered that over-promise and under-deliver, in many cases not even having a presence in the countries on whose laws they are attempting to provide counsel. It was in this context that the NRC agreed to proceed cautiously, first through a pilot project in Jordan prior to considering expanding the partnership to other jurisdictions. It was only after Dentons proved itself that the NRC overcame its initial skepticism and enthusiastically embraced expanding our partnership to other jurisdictions.

4. Observations

If there is anything I have learned from the practice of law, it is that there are two sides to every story. In this section, I present my views on the humanitarian sector partnership culture. My hope is that the perspective presented herein would be read in conjunction with that of the UN and NGOs when formulating and evaluating partnership policies.

Some might suggest that as someone who is formally outside of the international humanitarian sector, I am not qualified to offer my views on this controversial but important subject. After all, who am I to recommend to humanitarian organizations which policies they should adopt, which companies they should partner with or which organizations they should eschew? I do not face the challenges they must tackle on a daily basis; I do not know their financial state and needs; who am I then to critique their due diligence procedures and reputational risk analyses?

While I certainly do not claim to have a monopoly on the best ideas or practices for partnerships with the private sector, I am certain that the humanitarian sector ignores the views of private-sector actors, such as those presented herein, at its own peril. A dialogue with the private sector cannot be sidestepped or ignored. The fact that private sector funding accounts for only five or ten percent of the funds of some of the larger, government-funded humanitarian organizations does not justify shutting out private sector voices; the fact that funds are insufficient in addressing current overwhelming needs makes it all the more imperative that the humanitarian sector engage the private sector as partners.

I believe that it is critical that the humanitarian sector lends its ears to the views of the other side of the spectrum. It is in this spirit that I offer up my views in this chapter, views of a private sector actor who has forged partnerships with the humanitarian sector, some with success and others that died at the proposal stage. While my views may not be palatable to some readers, I hope the questions I raise and the candor with which I address the issues might trigger dialogue and shed light on how UN and NGO policies that govern partnerships so often have the unintended consequence of impeding partnerships that could have otherwise flourished with a lasting and positive impact on disaster-stricken communities.

a) Overview

Humanitarian agencies are under enormous pressure. Conflict and persecution have forced more people to flee their homes today than at any other time in recorded history.[62] Faced with the greatest humanitarian crisis of the 21st century and the greatest displacement of persons in history, humanitarian agencies are forced to address tremendous needs with limited resources. It is critical that humanitarian agencies reconsider the architecture of partnerships with the private sector. No longer is it acceptable to erect walls or draw dividing lines between the humanitarian and private sectors. The time is high to replace these walls with bridges.

Innumerable companies are eager to lend knowledge, expertise and material support to relieve the suffering of innocents. Most law firms encourage their lawyers' engagement in CSR initiatives by counting up to 100 hours dedicated to pro bono legal counselling towards bonus targets; many firms even require their attorneys to engage in pro bono services in order to receive a bonus. There is enormous potential for cooperation with the private sector. In my view, the humanitarian sector needs to seriously consider an architecture that more readily taps into the resources that the private sector has to offer, that absorbs volunteership offers and private sector assistance and properly channels the aspirations of private actors and companies to contribute towards the assistance of refugees.

b) Reconsidering Due Diligence Procedures

One of the first impediments to potential partnerships that I believe we should reconsider are the ethical guidelines for partnerships with the corporate sector and private foundations. I am by no means suggesting that international humanitarian agencies partner with organizations that fail to respect fundamental rights, counter-terrorism measures or the environment. As a lawyer, I am all too aware of the need to turn down potential sources of income due to ethical considerations. For new clients that approach Dentons,

---

[62] "Worldwide displacement hits all-time high as war and persecution increase," UNHCR, The UN Refugee Agency (18 June 2015). See also *World at War: UNHCR Global Trends: Forced Displacement in* 2014, UNHCR, The UN Refugee Agency (2014), available at <http://unhcr.org/556725e69.html>.

we run thorough conflicts searches and conduct due diligences to verify the identity of clients and the nature and purpose of the intended business relationship, in line with anti-money laundering laws and regulations. I am well aware of the burden of this process, especially for clients based in the Middle East, and the amount of constitutional documents needing to be reviewed before a potential client can engage our firm.

However, there is a difference between turning down potential partners in order to ensure security and the protection of fundamental values and turning down offers on the basis of the arbitrary application of subjective criteria. Nowhere is the arbitrary nature of subjective criteria made clearer than in the vetting process of UN agencies, where some private companies pass the vetting process of one UN agency, only to then be denied by another UN agency. For example, both UNICEF and the WFP are UN organs falling under the General Assembly. Ostensibly, they should have the same standards with respect to the review of potential partners from a reputation, ethics and integrity perspective. Yet on countless occasions, companies have been denied WFP partnership status, only to then be approved as UNICEF partners. As an attorney from the WFP's largest donor nation, I am forced to question the rationale behind the Programme's partnership vetting process, particularly in light of the countless refugees I have encountered who complain of hunger and a lack of food following WFP budget cuts. Wouldn't the WFP be more effective in eliminating hunger if it were more open to private sector pro bono assistance offers, thus permitting it to dedicate more funds to programming?

c) Reconsidering Reputational Risk Analysis

Some humanitarian organizations go as far as denying funds from potential partners because of a concern that associating with such partners can taint the recipient organization's brand. Consider, for example, the case of Médecins Sans Frontières (**MSF**), which denied a USD 500,000 donation from McDonald's in Niger out of a concern that the juxtaposition of the McDonald's logo against that of MSF would tarnish the latter's image.

MSF is viewed by many in the humanitarian community as an organization that sets the gold standard for impartiality, neutrality and independence. For example, following the destruction of an MSF hospital in Kunduz, Afghanistan, by US military forces in 2015, MSF refused to accept funds from the US government to reconstruct the hospital.[63] Because the US government was a party to the Afghan conflict, MSF reasoned that accepting funds from the government would compromise MSF's neutrality, at least in the eyes of the Afghan beneficiaries that the organization served.

[63] The US government acknowledged its breach of international humanitarian law in carrying out the attack, which, according to MSF, left immobile patients burning in their beds, staff decapitated by shrapnel and "people running while on fire and then falling unconscious on the ground." Médecins Sans Frontières, "Public release of initial MSF internal review," MSF International Office, Geneva (5 Nov. 2015), p. 10.

While refusing to accept funding from a State party to a conflict makes sense from a neutrality-preservation perspective, the rationale behind refusing half a million dollars from McDonalds to assist children in Niger baffles me. Certainly, McDonalds is no "elite" brand. But is preserving an elite image any concern to children dying of preventable disease? Of course, reputations are to be cherished and protected, and potential partners should be carefully vetted, as scandals could implicate and tarnish the reputations of partner humanitarian organization. But where do we draw the line? What private sector actor has not been without its share of scandals? If in our quest for private sector partners we insist on working with only those saints that have never been subject to any scandals, investigations, inquiries, disputes or litigation, our pool of potential private sector partners will completely dry out. Where would thousands of displaced persons who will benefit from Ikea's ingenious USD 1,000 solar-powered flat-pack refugee shelter be if UNHCR refused to partner with Ikea because a due diligence investigation uncovered a financial, political or tax scandal in Ikea's distant past?

D. Opening Minds to Partnerships

Once we have torn down the false dichotomy between "humanitarian saints and capitalist villains" in the culture of so many aid agencies,[64] private companies and other organizations will have a green light to partner with humanitarian agencies in delivering much needed aid and assistance. First, a series of misconceptions on the nature of partnerships must be dismissed.

1. Effective Partnerships Do Not Need to be Established on a Large Scale

Partnerships do not need to be established on a large scale to be effective. Perhaps you are a dentist who owns your own clinic. You could pack up your equipment and make your next vacation the Beqa' Valley of Lebanon, distributing equipment, teaching dental hygiene and giving free dental cleanings. A partner organization could potentially assist in overcoming the language barrier and obtaining any necessary permits. While a one or two week medical mission is not on its own going to make a significant impact in the refugee crisis, such initiatives when approached in the aggregate by engaged citizens from the world over do have an impact. In addition to potentially providing medical care, food, supplies and education, such small-scale interventions go a long way in restoring hope and showing refugees that the world has not forgotten them.

In my visits to Syrian refugee camps across the Middle East, I have been able to participate in the distribution of educational supplies, books, toys and cash assistance. Time and again, I found that refugees appreciated the time and attention they were being given more than anything material I could hand out. In my visits to camps, families would invite me to their tents and would delight at the opportunity to share their stories. Though they had little to give,

[64] Elise Bijon, presentation at the NRC Global Corporate Partnerships Seminar, Dubai, United Arab Emirates (1 Dec. 2015).

they would offer me tea and coffee and invite me to join them in sharing what little bread they had. Children would give me toys and candy. One girl at a refugee camp school wanted me to have her only sippy cup.

In December of 2015, I had an opportunity to participate in the distribution of wooden stars painted by Dentons lawyers and staff in New York and children at My Little School in Riyadh with words of encouragement to Syrian refugees. The stars, distributed in partnership with the New York Says Thank You Foundation's Stars of Hope program, impart messages of hope and healing, such as "courage," "dream" and "friendship." I distributed the Stars of Hope at Kawergosk Refugee Camp for Syrian refugees and at an Iraqi camp for internally-displaced Yazidis. As I gave each child a star, their eyes lit up as though I had given them a priceless treasure. After I had completed distributing the Stars, the children did not turn around and ask for food or money. Their only demand was that I stay and play with them. As I learned from this and many other experiences, merely showing kindness and attention to these children is as important as feeding and clothing them; in meeting physical needs we should not overlook the equally-important emotional needs.

Syrian refugee children at Kawergosk Refugee Camp in Iraq pose with stars painted by Dentons lawyers and staff in New York and children in Riyadh.

In one of my visits to Syrian refugee camps, I participated in the distribution of USD 10,000, which is the amount required to construct shelters for seven refugee families. This figure may seem paltry in light of the 4.3 million registered Syrian refugees. Yet we should never look at individual intervention in isolation. When thousands of individuals team up to intervene, when thousands of USD 10,000 donations are added together, when thousands of advocates each commit to raise USD 10,000 or even USD 100,000, the ripple effects are enormous. There are perhaps millions of advocates having no formal affiliation with humanitarian agencies who on their own are finding ways to contribute to the relief of Syrian refugees. If all of these advocates concluded that their contribution, in isolation, would have no impact on the global refugee crisis, then indeed, they would desist and no impact would be felt. But small-scale interventions on a global scale can and do noticeably impact the well-being of refugees, and I constantly see this in my visits to camps. The footprint of advocates who came before me—whether it was the new shoes donated by TOMS to Syrian refugee children or the new school built at Ankawa 2 Camp–are always visible.

2. Geography Should Be No Restriction

A company does not need to be operating in the Middle East to be able to provide assistance, relief or protection to Syrian refugees. In fact, the need for knowledge and expertise in jurisdictions as remote as Canada, Japan, the United Kingdom or the United States is just as great as it is in Lebanon, Jordan or Iraq. Years ago, it was possible to say that the Syrian refugee crisis was a regional phenomenon, impacting only Syria's neighboring countries. Today, the crisis has become global, impacting every country in which Syrian refugees have sought asylum. Central Europe and the Balkan Peninsula—particularly Greece—have been especially impacted, but the refugee crisis extends to Egypt and across North Africa, Eastern Europe, Germany and across Western Europe and throughout North America. Every country that has agreed to resettle Syrian refugees, nations as geographically diverse as Argentina, Australia, Brazil, Canada, France, Germany, Sweden, the United States, the United Kingdom, Uruguay and Venezuela, must now struggle with how to integrate a foreign people with a distinct language, heritage, culture and (in many cases) religion into a culture that is new to them.

It is not necessary to travel to the Middle East to assist Syrian refugees when many are being resettled in our own neighborhoods. It is possible to assist refugees by partnering with local organizations that are providing refugees with housing and employment. Many of these organizations may demand the same types of services that Dentons provides the NRC in the Middle East. For example:

- A humanitarian aid agency in Canada may wish to understand the rights of asylum seekers under local law;

- An organization in the United Kingdom might seek to register as a charity;
- An NGO in Brazil may seek to train resettled Syrians on their housing, land and property rights under local law;
- A non-profit organization in the United States might require assistance in completing an application to the Internal Revenue Service for status as a tax-exempt 501(c)(3) organization.

These are just a few examples of opportunities private law firms have in assisting Syrian refugees without ever having an employee set foot in the Middle East. The possibilities for companies in other sectors are similarly boundless.

3. An Entity Does not Need to be a Company to be a Humanitarian Partner

It is not necessary to be a company to partner with the UN or humanitarian agencies. The type of potential partner is limited only by one's aptitude for creative thinking.

- Teachers at public schools can contact humanitarian agencies to set up summer camps with volunteers, teaching refugee children anything from math and science to theatre and performing arts. If language is a barrier, such camps can focus on subjects that transcend language barriers, such as the visual arts, music, sports or foreign languages such as English or French, which further skills that may later prove essential for employment.
- A hospital employee can explore which supply stock items are in excess and organize a medical drive to donate supplies to medical agencies working with Syrian refugees such as Médecins Sans Frontières (Doctors Without Borders), the ICRC or the International Medical Corps.
- A member of a local city council might have the leverage to launch a sister city initiative, pairing up with one of Syria's neighboring cities such as Amman, Beirut, Irbid or Erbil, to coordinate humanitarian assistance or prepare for the receipt of Syrian refugees for local resettlement.

Over the past years, as I visited refugee camps and wrote this book, countless friends and concerned family members asked how they could contribute and help Syrian refugees. Time and again, I realized that the greatest impediment to effectively delivering aid and assistance to Syrian refugees is not human indifference to suffering. Rather, it is the inability of the humanitarian and the private sectors to come together to harness the talents, skills and resources of private companies and individuals and effectively channel their energy to the relief of refugee beneficiaries. The first step to establishing effective partnerships is rethinking the current humanitarian framework and the unnecessary or outmoded impediments to partnerships. In opening our minds as to how the private sector can more effectively participate in humanitarian relief, we will erase an unnecessary dividing line between the humanitarian and private sectors and thereby permit the private sector to step up its engagement in humanitarian response.

Chapter 8. Taking Action: Civil Society Initiatives

A. Overview

More than 11 million Syrians—half the country—are in need of life-saving assistance this year alone. Millions have fled Syria and are living in overcrowded camps with limited resources. Demands for assistance eclipse what humanitarian agencies and governments are able to provide. It is critical that civil society organizations, civic associations and private individuals and companies step in to fill this gap. Humanitarian agencies need our time and talents as much as they need our financial support. There is no limit to the types of assistance that private initiatives can contribute, provided that individuals and enterprises act creatively and with an open and entrepreneurial spirit.

B. Partnerships through Employers

As discussed in the previous chapter, one approach to assisting Syrian refugees is establishing partnerships with humanitarian agencies through one's employer, business or civic organization, whether it is through fundraising, setting up matching funds programs or making in-kind contributions of goods, supplies, knowledge or expertise. Such partnerships can take a wide variety of forms, whether one's employer is a company, NGO or other not-for-profit entity, educational institution or governmental body. Even civic and faith-based organizations can find ways to partner by raising funds or sending volunteers or in-kind donations.

One limitation to the potential for establishing partnerships remains a view among many in the humanitarian community that the private sector has no role to play in humanitarian relief. Consequently, many actors in the humanitarian sphere rebuff cooperation with the private sector. In the view of these actors, the only contribution fit for the private sector is the financing of humanitarian relief efforts through cash donations. As discussed in the previous chapter and aptly summarized by Elise Bijon, the World Food Programme's Private Partnerships Manager for the Middle East, North Africa, Eastern Europe and Central Asia, the only way to progress past this impediment is to tear down the false dichotomy between "humanitarian saints and capitalist villains" in the culture of so many aid agencies.[65] We all have a role to play—the private sector included—in positively impacting our communities and relieving the suffering of those impacted by war and

---

[65] *Id.*

disaster. It is only after we replace walls between the private and humanitarian sectors that the latter can fully tap into the enormous resources—both financial and technical—that the private sector has to offer.

C. Volunteering

1. Overview

Volunteering is a second way to contribute one's time and talents to assisting Syrian refugees. If you believe a volunteer needs to be an expert in refugee issues in order to assist Syrian refugees, think again. Consider the team of three volunteers at Atmeh Refugee Camp, which in 2013 had employed three volunteers to begin each day at 5:30 am preparing a late afternoon meal for Syrian refugees. These three volunteers, working out of a single kitchen with a mud floor, tin roof and cement walls with gaping holes in it, managed to feed 17,000 refugees each day.[66] Whatever your talents or skills, a willing disposition coupled with a commitment to assist the vulnerable and dispossessed can make a significant impact in the protection of Syrian refugees.

One limitation with volunteering, however, is that opportunities will generally only be open to students with long summer breaks or professionals who are able to take extensive sabbaticals from their work, since most organizations require a commitment of at least eight to ten weeks from potential volunteers. This is not because such organizations do not value shorter term volunteerships; rather, it is because of a longstanding view that the dividends of volunteerships only start to pay out after the first several weeks of the volunteership. Before that, the host organization pays out significant administrative costs in recruiting and training volunteers. Many humanitarian organizations thus insist that volunteers commit a minimum of two months, after which point the benefits derived from volunteerships begin to exceed the cost involved in setting up volunteerships by way of staff time, administration and logistics.

With that being said, however, there are several organizations that accept volunteers for shorter-term assignments. Relief & Reconciliation for Syria AISBL, for example, accepts international volunteers to assist in organizing and implementing educational and recreational activities for children and adolescents of Syrian refugee and Lebanese host communities. The association takes on volunteers for as little as one to two weeks for its summer camps, cross-country games, sport competitions and work-shops in theatre, photography and music. It may also be possible to submit one's name to lists of pro bono legal services maintained by some organizations, such as the International Rescue Committee (**IRC**). In such cases, attorneys will be called on a case-by-case basis to provide their expertise on

---

[66] Tobin, Sara A., *The Syrian Refugee Crisis and Lessons from the Iraqi Refugee Experience*, Boston University Institute for Iraqi Studies (2013), p. 12.

immigration law without having to relocate or commit several weeks on end to volunteer on a full-time basis.

2. Opportunities

Following is a list of organizations that accept volunteers on an unpaid basis. The list is not intended to be exhaustive but rather to provide a sense of the range and diversity of available opportunities to volunteer in the assistance and protection of Syrian refugees.

a) Hand in Hand for Syria

Hand in Hand for Syria is a British not-for-profit organization that was established soon after the Syrian conflict began in 2011. The organization brings medical and humanitarian aid into 90% of Syria and implements aid funded by, and on behalf of, some of the world's largest aid agencies.

Hand in Hand for Syria accepts medical professionals, including doctors, nurses and specialists with skills relevant to conflict zones, to volunteer in Syria. It also accepts volunteers in the United Kingdom to assist with events, fundraising, packing and sorting, translation, administration, press and publicity. Moreover, Hand in Hand for Syria seeks delivery drivers to take local aid donations from within the United Kingdom as well as convoy drivers within Syria.

*b) International Refugee Assistance Project (**IRAP**)*

The International Refugee Assistance Project (**IRAP**) organizes law students and lawyers to develop and enforce a set of legal and human rights for refugees and displaced persons. Mobilizing direct legal aid and systemic policy advocacy, IRAP serves the world's most persecuted individuals to empower the next generation of human rights leaders.

IRAP seeks volunteer attorneys in its New York, Amman and Beirut offices to work directly with refugees in the Middle East and assist IRAP staff and attorneys with the screening and preparation of legal cases. Volunteers gain valuable experience, including:

- Conducting initial intake interviews with clients, and drafting intake reports;
- Providing direct representation in UNHCR refugee status determination, US Special Immigrant Visa and USCIS refugee interviews and proceedings, including accompanying refugees to interviews;
- Preparing affidavits and other evidence;
- Researching factual and legal claims; and
- Drafting memoranda and briefs.

Volunteers wishing to assist with legal advocacy or interested in working on cases or supervising law students may reach IRAP by writing to info@refugeerights.org.

c) *International Rescue Committee (**IRC**)*

The International Rescue Committee (**IRC**) is a global humanitarian aid, relief and development non-governmental organization founded in 1933. The IRC offers emergency aid and long-term assistance to refugees and those displaced by war, persecution or natural disaster. Currently working in over 40 countries and 22 cities in the US, the IRC resettles refugees and helps them become self-sufficient.

The IRC accepts volunteers into its programs in the following US cities: Atlanta, GA; Baltimore, MD; Boise, ID; Charlottesville, VA; Dallas, TX; Los Angeles, CA; Miami, FL; New York, NY / Elizabeth, NJ; Northern California, CA; Phoenix, AZ; Salt Lake City, UT; San Diego, CA; Seattle, WA; Silver Spring, MD; Tuscon, AZ; and Wichita, KS. Volunteers may engage in a variety of activities, including: mentoring refugee families and individuals; assisting refugees to develop effective job seeking and interview results; and helping maintain community gardens.

d) *Mercy Corps*

Mercy Corps is an American aid agency engaged in transitional environments that have experienced natural disaster, economic collapse or conflict. Its employees are mobilized to deliver food and supplies and enable people to rebuild their economies with community-driven and market-led programs. To lay the groundwork for longer-term recovery, Mercy Corps focuses on connecting to both government and business for the changes they would like to implement.

Mercy Corps offers volunteers opportunities at its global headquarters in Portland, Oregon. Volunteers are able to get involved in administration, community fundraising and the Mercy Corps Action Center and MicroMentor, There are also occasionally opportunities for individuals to support international programming through internships.

e) *Relief & Reconciliation for Syria*

Relief & Reconciliation for Syria AISBL (www.reliefandreconciliation.org) is an international NGO organized as an *association internationale sans but lucratif* (international non-profit organization) under Belgian law. Combining peacebuilding with humanitarian aid for those affected by the Syrian crisis, Relief & Reconciliation for Syria unites diverse communities in advocating for the future of the Syrian youth. The organization opened its first Peace Centre in a small village in northern Lebanon, just seven miles from the Syrian border, welcoming Syrian and Lebanese youth of different confessions and groups and providing psychosocial, educational and material support to newly arriving Syrian refugees. Since 2013, Relief & Reconciliation for Syria has operated a non-formal refugee camp school in Akkar, northern Lebanon, providing education to hundreds of children from surrounding camps who have been out of school since their displacement from Syria.

Relief & Reconciliation for Syria AISBL accepts international volunteers to assist in implementing an innovative approach to assisting the Syrian refugee crisis in Lebanon. As part of an ethos of bringing people together, international volunteers combine forces with local volunteers in organizing and implementing educational and recreational activities for children and adolescents of Syrian refugee and Lebanese host communities. Volunteers may commit to teach workshops of one to two weeks or may commit to longer volunteerships of up to one academic year, teaching children sports, arts and languages, organizing interreligious solidarity events, cross-country games, sport competitions, summer camps and regular work-shops in theatre, photography and music.

f) SEED Foundation

SEED Foundation (**SEED**), a local NGO, is one of many civil society initiatives working for development in Kurdistan. SEED's mission is to promote social, educational and economic development, to address humanitarian needs, and promote and protect human rights across the Kurdistan Region of Iraq.

Among its recent projects, SEED established a new psycho-social services center in Mamilyan Camp in Akre, around a two-hour drive north of Erbil. The camp shelters almost 13,000 internally displaced Iraqis, approximately 80% of whom belong to the Yazidi minority group, who fled Sinjar and Mosul to escape the brutal takeover of those areas by IS. Given the almost unimaginable abuses perpetrated against the Yazidi community, rates of trauma in the camp are high. SEED provides much-needed psychotherapy and social-work services, as well as training, education and recreation opportunities to those in need, with a focus on Yazidi women and girls who are survivors of sexual violence.

SEED accepts volunteers on short-term bases, provided volunteers' needs match up with SEED's programs.

g) Syrian-American Medical Society (SAMS) Foundation

The Syrian-American Medical Society (**SAMS**) Foundation seeks to harness the talents of Syrian-American healthcare professionals and channel them toward medical relief for the people of Syria and the United States. SAMS has established and supports various medical facilities and specialty care clinics, including field hospitals, advanced medical points, trauma facilities and psychosocial centers. In addition, SAMS provides education and training and advocates for delivery of humanitarian aid, protection of healthcare professionals and facilities and easing administrative restrictions on sending medications, medical consumables and equipment.

The Foundation provides potential volunteers opportunities to take part in a wide variety of advocacy activities, including participating in medical missions, hosting events, donating, raising funds and starting local SAMS chapters.

h) United Nations Volunteer (UNV) Programme

The United Nations Volunteers (**UNV**) programme promotes voluntary service to support peace and development worldwide. UNV mobilizes more than 7,500 volunteers for development projects around the world every year and it operates a special service to connect development organizations with volunteers worldwide through the internet (UNV Online Volunteering service).

Foreign language skills are highly sought after by the UNV Online Volunteering service, which includes opportunities to assist a host of UN agencies such as UNICEF and UNESCO in translating training materials into French, Spanish, Arabic and other foreign languages.

D. Donating and Fundraising

In the case of the busy executive or successful entrepreneur who has disposable income but not disposable time, donating to humanitarian agencies may be the best way to partner in the assistance and protection of Syrian refugees.

For creative entrepreneurs and savvy businesspersons who can effectively deliver a pitch, fundraising for humanitarian organizations will come naturally and multiply the power of their capacity to personally donate. Many organizations make it simple to partner with them to help raise funds. The Norwegian Refugee Council, for example, allows potential partners to start their own fundraisers by clicking a link right on the organization's homepage. The web platform allows users to launch a fundraiser through just a few simple clicks, giving partners the ability to choose whether to earmark funds to help families fleeing war in the Syria region or to support the NRC's work more generally.

Other organizations send materials such as DVDs with feature films or documentaries that can be used to host screenings at a home, library or community center as a fundraising platform. This strategy is employed by World Vision, which sends a kit comprised of DVDs of the documentary *Journey to Jamaa*, which can be screened by partners to share the importance of child sponsorship. Free kits include fact sheets, books and photos of children awaiting sponsorship, all of which can be distributed at screenings of the feature film. My wife and I were so moved by this film that we subsequently sponsored a child in Mexico.

E. Going Solo

1. Overview

It is not necessary to partner with a humanitarian aid organization in order to deliver assistance to Syrian refugees; it is possible to go solo. Again, the possibilities here are limited only by one's imagination. Whether it is raising awareness through a book or a blog, reaching out to and welcoming individual Syrian families that have resettled in our communities or writing letters to elected officials to expand resettlement programs, individual initiatives can be just as effective as partnerships if they are properly planned.

2. "Solidarity Tourism" and Humanitarian Missions

Solidarity tourism is an innovative way of traveling that combines volunteering and tourism. It is a controversial form of humanitarian aid because it has the potential of becoming a form of "watching" and "seeing" the victims of conflict or natural disaster without actually offering any real aid. Such an empty form of "intervention"—if it can even be given this name—is not what I have in mind in discussing this section. Rather, I am referring to solidarity tourism when done right, when volunteers and local populations are brought together around the common purpose of supporting the development of the local community and its economy—a way of traveling that can enable new encounters with diverse cultures while promoting international solidarity and service. When approached in this way, solidarity tourism has the potential to make a lasting and positive impact on communities.

A solidarity tourist invests most of his or her time and funds in a local development project, thus giving her the opportunity to leave a mark in the local community and return to her country of origin with indelible memories. Moreover, solidarity tourism channels tourists' funds to countries and communities often struggling with poverty, underdevelopment or under the burden of humanitarian crises, thus serving as an investment in these economies, rather than to traditional vacation resorts.

A busy professional with two weeks of vacation might have the option of spending those two weeks at a luxurious beach resort in some corner of the world. But he also has the choice of instead investing his funds in the Syrian refugees and in the communities that are hosting them. He might, for example, opt to buy his plane ticket to Beirut and then spend his two weeks among Syrian refugees living in the Beqa' Valley. During his time, he might volunteer in a workshop or in a summer camp, organizing sport competitions and similar activities that in the aggregate will help restore normalcy to the lives of refugee children by building trust and fostering relationships in safe and secure environments where children impacted by war can learn and thrive.

Volunteer teachers are in great demand as hundreds of thousands of children living in informal tented settlements have been left outside of the formal schooling systems of their host communities.

Solidarity tourism has the potential of making a lasting and positive impact in the countries hosting Syrian refugees. Many of these countries are already strained with water scarcity, rising energy prices and joblessness. If half a million tourists were to opt for solidarity tourism in Lebanon, Jordan and Iraqi Kurdistan each year, it would have an enormous positive impact on the local economies and would promote job growth and social and economic development.

Moreover, if solidarity tourists divert funds that otherwise would have gone into expensive resorts or luxurious hotels, instead using these funds to purchase clothing, food and medicine for Syrian refugees, solidarity tourism would carry with it the potential to bring relief to countless refugees.[67]

One can be very creative in approaching volunteering. A professional with two weeks of vacation to spare can get in touch with one of the NGOs working with Syrian refugee children such as Save the Children or Relief & Reconciliation for Syria and ask how to organize a workshop teaching children sports, arts, theatre, music or languages.

Of course, there are safety and security considerations that must be taken into account before traveling abroad, especially to disaster-stricken nations. Before organizing a humanitarian mission, it is imperative that the traveler review warnings and travel advisories published by embassies operating in the country to which he is traveling.

3. Case Study: Humanitarians Rasha Hatab and Aya Arkadan in Action

a) Overview

On 2 November 2015, Rasha Hatab and Aya Arkadan began a campaign using the crowdfunding platform GoFundMe to raise funds for a Syrian refugee humanitarian relief project.

As she explained on her funding appeal, Rasha Hatab spent every summer with her grandparents and cousins in Syria since she was eight years old. She recounts her memories of a country that "lived in perfect harmony," with people of all religious backgrounds peacefully coexisting. Having read about the plight of Syrian refugees and their desperate state as they cross into Europe via the Greek islands, she felt moved to take action. In her appeal, she wrote[68]:

> As a mother, I want to believe that if I were in this situation, ... other people would take action. I am an average person leading a very average life who wants to believe that one person's desire to take action can make an impact. Please help me make an impact.

Rasha and Aya sought to move family and friends to donate to a campaign that would enable them to purchase basic necessities, including children's Tylenol, baby formula, hand wipes, undergarments and diapers to take with them on a field visit to Greece to distribute to Syrian refugees. Once on the ground, they used funds to purchase shoes, clothes and food locally

---

[67] If solidarity tourism is accompanied by the distribution of funds or other forms of material aid, it is important that the solidarity tourist bring enough of whatever is being distributed to reach every member of the target community. For example, if a solidarity tourist raises enough funds to purchase 200 pairs of shoes, the distribution should be made in a small informal settlement where every member of the community will receive a pair of shoes, rather than at a camp hosting 80,000 refugees, where the receipt of some but not all members of the community carries with it the potential of triggering unnecessary tensions.

[68] "Syrian Refugees Greece," GoFundMe, available at <https://www.gofundme.com/hy84fcvg> (last accessed 21 Dec. 2015).

for distribution. All donations would go to Syrian refugees, as Rasha and Aya planned on paying their own personal expenses relating to travel and accommodation.

Within just one month, Rasha and Aya managed to meet their goal by raising USD 15,000 for Syrian refugees. Donations ranging from USD 20 to USD 500, with an average of USD 100, were made by 143 individuals, some of whom did not know Rasha and Aya directly but only heard of them through common contacts.

b) Lessons Learned

Rasha and Aya's mission is remarkable on several levels. First, it demonstrates an innovative approach to humanitarian action driven by individuals rather than governments or large organizations. Being planned and managed at a local level by individuals without institutional affiliations, humanitarian action has the flexibility to quickly deploy and adapt to changing circumstances without being impeded by the bureaucratic decision-making processes inherent to governments and large organizations. An example of this was Rasha's decision to distribute a portion of the aid collected to Syrian refugees in camps on the Syrian-Turkish border after a route diversion led her to discover that the funds would have more of an impact given the desperate state of refugees just across the Turkish border.[69]

Second, the mission demonstrates the remarkable ability of a self-described "average person" to raise a significant sum of money in a relatively short period of time, simply by publishing a funding appeal online outlining how funds would be spent. Because Rasha and Aya reached out to friends and family, an already-existing platform of trust obviated the need to extensively justify or provide detailed accounts as to how funds would be spent. NGOs that rely on government funding, in contrast, often find themselves bogged down by extensive accounting and reporting that prevent them from focusing all of their efforts on their mission.

Finally, Rasha and Aya's mission highlights the potential of grassroots action as an effective advocacy and fundraising tool that far too many humanitarian organizations ignore. While many organizations focus on large grants by a few institutional donors, they often overlook the hundreds or thousands of smaller donations that can easily come in if they directly tap into civil society. A humanitarian NGO or international organization such as the UN can attract such donations by simply setting up a platform on its web site that allows fellow advocates to fundraise on behalf of a cause being sponsored by the NGO or organization. The very same platform that Rasha and Aya used to fundraise USD 15,000 in one month can be adopted and adapted by NGOs to partner with potential advocates. Such a platform can give partners from the private sector with a heart for humanitarian work an opportunity to directly support the work of NGOs without having to leave the

---

[69] Update #7, "Syrian Refugees Greece," GoFundMe, available at <https://www.gofundme.com/hy84fcvg> (last accessed 22 Dec. 2015).

private sector. To further promote the partnership, NGOs and UN agencies can designate partners that raise funds above a specified threshold as "affiliates" or "advocates" that may undertake a field visit to a refugee camp or informal settlement where they can witness first-hand the relief being administered as a result of their fundraising efforts.

Chapter 9. Conclusion: Giving Children Hope and a Future

The burden of caring for refugees should not fall on governments, international agencies and charitable organizations acting alone. As the Syrian refugee crisis demonstrates with terrible clarity, the ability of governments and humanitarian organizations to find a durable solution to the refugee crisis and provide assistance and protection until such durable solutions are found is extremely limited. The private sector cannot sit believing that the care of refugees is the sole responsibility of the UN or of charitable organizations, when the desperate needs of Syrian refugees far exceed what the UN and charitable organizations are able to provide. Many humanitarian agencies are in a triage state, allocating aid on the basis of severity while the needs of others are neglected. This has especially become the case in 2015, where the rapid deterioration of Syria's security has doubled the number of refugees in Turkey alone.

The private sector, with all of the knowledge, expertise, creativity and financial and material resources it has at its disposal, cannot sit by idly expecting governments and large international organizations to act, especially when small companies and private initiatives have the flexibility to quickly deploy and react to humanitarian crisis, while governments and large organizations so often remain deadlocked in exceedingly burdensome decision-making processes. Nor is it acceptable for the humanitarian community to rebuff private sector partnership offers on the basis that the private sector is not specialized in humanitarian relief; one should not require specialized diploma in order to coordinate the logistics of food consignments, of assisting refugees in finding housing and employment, in advocating for expanded resettlement programs or in working side-by-side with international agencies in delivering humanitarian aid. In developing a response that extends beyond the provision of food security, clean water and medical assistance and education, we will see that everyone has something to offer—if a multinational law firm such as Dentons has a role to play in alleviating the suffering of the Syrian people, then surely, there is a role for every company to play.

Given the magnitude of the Syrian refugee crisis, it is unacceptable for the humanitarian community or the private sector to draw a dividing line between the private and public sectors or to narrowly circumscribe the bailiwick of either sector. Private companies operating in the Middle East ignore the refugee crisis to their own peril; if such companies are committed to their own futures in the region, then so too must they be committed to promoting long-term stability in the Middle Eastern communities in which their employees live and work.

The Syrian refugee crisis reminds us that there are problems beyond our borders, bigger than our own communities and more important than our short-term financial balance sheets. The private sector cannot choose to ignore the role it has to play in humanitarian emergencies such as the Syrian refugee crisis, unless we choose to allow the legacy of our inaction to be an entire generation of Syrians deprived of basic rights and opportunity for advancement.

This chapter has demonstrated the myriad ways that ordinary individuals not directly linked with the humanitarian field can contribute to the assistance and protection of Syrian refugees. We all have a role to play.

If we are to rediscover our humanity, if we truly value human life, if we are to call ourselves committed humanitarians, then we will unequivocally answer the moral call and ethical duty to act. Whether it is through establishing partnerships through private companies, volunteering, donating, fundraising or going solo with fresh initiatives, the Syrian refugee crisis gives humanity a chance to act—to restore human dignity to the victims of the conflict, to seek justice for the needy, to defend orphans, to plead for widows and visit the needy in their distress. Together, through collective action, we can send a loud message to the Syrian people, one that overpowers the deafening silence of our inaction in Rwanda, or our indifference to the Holocaust until it was too late, one that boldly declares to the Syrian people: Do not fear, Be not discouraged, All is not over!

Building on this foundation, I invite the reader: Whether it is through your workplace, through your contacts in government, media or education, through your wealth, your entrepreneurial spirit, your artistic abilities or professional skills—whether in administration, engineering, finance, law, medicine, marketing or teaching—join me in putting your gifts, talents and skills to work for the Syrian people. Join me in restoring hope and a future to the people of Syria.

In joining Syrian refugees in rebuilding their country and reclaiming their dreams, even when it costs us our own comfort and security, even when it means enduring all things, even risking our lives, we can—we will!—restore the hope of the Syrian people and revive their faith in the future. In sowing bountifully, we will reap bountifully, for seeds of hope generously planted will yield a generous harvest—a bright future, a world that guarantees the dignity and worth of the Syrian people and secures their fundamental freedoms and inalienable rights; one that asserts that Syrians are our brothers and sisters as members of the human family; a world based on the bedrocks of justice and peace, where governments respect human rights and the rule of law and are founded on the principles of the dignity and worth of the individual; one where children are not wrenched from their parents by barbarous acts of violence, but rather, are raised by their families in safe, happy environments; one where children know peace rather than war, kindness rather than cruelty, plenty rather than famine; a world marked by a spirit of brotherhood rather than a spirit of fear, where love overcomes all things.

Appendices

Bibliography

Susan Akram, Sarah Bidinger, Aaron Lang, Danielle Hites, Yoana Kuzmova, Elena Noureddine (authors), Lys Runnerstrom, Timothy Kistner (contributors), "Protecting Syrian Refugees: Laws, Policies, and Global Responsibility Sharing," 7 *Middle East Law and Governance*, 287 (2015).

John Balouziyeh, *Principles of International Law* (Vandeplas Publishing, 2012).

Rex Brynen and Bassel F. Salloukh, eds. 2004. *Persistent Permeability? Regionalism, Localism, and Globalization in the Middle East.* Burlington, VT: Ashgate Publishing Limited.

Russell Chapman, *Syria: Refugees and Rebels*, Russell Chapman (2014).

CIA World Factbook, United States Central Intelligence Agency, available at <https://www.cia.gov/cia/publications/factbook>.

Tom Clark, *The Global Refugee Regime: Charity, Management and Human Rights*, Trafford Publishing (Victoria, BC: 2004).

Committee on Foreign Affairs of the House of Representatives, *The Syrian Humanitarian Crisis: Four Years Later and No End in Sight*, CreateSpace Independent Publishing Platform (2015).

Convention and Protocol Relating to the Status of Refugees, United Nations High Commissioner for Refugees (2006).

Diego Cupolo, *SEVEN SYRIANS: War Accounts from Syrian Refugees*, 8th House Publishing (2013).

Reese Erlich, Noam Chomsky (Foreword), *Inside Syria: The Backstory of Their Civil War and What the World Can Expect*, Prometheus Books (2014).765

Erika Feller, Volker Turk, and Frances Nicholson, eds., *Refugee Protection in International Law: UNHCR's Global Consultations on International Protection*, Cambridge University Press (New York, NY: 2003).

Futures Under Threat: The impact of the education crisis on Syria's children, Save the Children (London: 2014).

Joshua Landis, *Syria Comment: Syrian Politics, History, and Religion* (http://www.joshualandis.com/blog.).

Ming Lauren Holden, *The Syria Dispatches: Literary Nonfiction about the Search for Syrian Refugees*, CreateSpace Independent Publishing Platform (2015).

Albert Hourani, *A History of the Arab Peoples,* The Belknap Press of Harvard University Press (Cambridge: 1991).

Sarah Kenyon Lischer, *Dangerous Sanctuaries: Refugee Camps, Civil War, and the Dilemmas of Humanitarian Aid*, Cornell University Press (Ithica, NY: 2005).

Karen Musalo, Jennifer Moore, and Richard A. Boswell. *Refugee Law and Policy: A Comparative and International Approach, 2nd Edition,* Carolina Academic Press (Durham, NC: 2002).

Safe Avenues to Asylum? The Actual and Potential Role of EU Diplomatic Representations in Processing Asylum Requests, United Nations High Commissioner for Refugees (2002).

Sara A. Tobin, *The Syrian Refugee Crisis and Lessons from the Iraqi Refugee Experience*, Boston University Institute for Iraqi Studies (2013).

UNCHR and International Protection: A Protection Induction Programme, United Nations High Commissioner for Refugees (2006).

Universal Declaration of Human Rights (1948), General Assembly Resolution 217 A (III). United Nations High Commissioner for Refugees, Division of External Relations (2006).

World Bank, *The Kurdistan Region of Iraq: Assessing the Economic and Social Impact of the Syrian Conflict and ISIS*, World Bank Publications (2015).

Ruben Zaiotti, "Dealing with non-Palestinian Refugees in the Middle East; Policies and Practices in an Uncertain Environment," *International Journal of Refugee Law* (2006).

Permissions Notices and Copyright Reservations

Humanitarian Agencies

Overview

The Syrian refugee crisis demonstrates the way a diverse cross-sector of UN agencies work together to provide humanitarian relief in tandem with governmental (*i.e.*, Jordanian) organizations and non-governmental organizations. The following is a sampling of humanitarian organizations active in providing assistance and protection to Syrian refugees in the Middle East:

Medical

- Médecins Sans Frontières (Doctors Without Borders)
- ICRC
- International Medical Corps
- French military field hospital
- Moroccan military field hospital
- Italian Field Hospital
- IOM

Water and Sanitation facilities

- German Federal Agency for Technical Relief (Bundesanstalt Technisches Hilfswerk)
- Swedish Civil Contingencies Agency (**MSB**)
- MercyCorps

Food / Shelter

- WFP
- UNHCR

Education

- NRC
- UNICEF
- Save the Children-Jordan
- IOM
- UNFPA

“We cannot do great things on this Earth, only small things with great love.”
Blessed Teresa of Calcutta
1910-1997

Made in the USA
Middletown, DE
04 October 2016